ARNULFO L. OLIVEIRA MEMORIAL LIBRARY
1825 MAY STREET
BROWNSVILLE, TEXAS 78520

RECHARGE YOUR CAREER & YOUR LIFE

**5 Best Ideas and
95 Activities That
Translate Into
Success and Renewal**

**By
Paul R. Timm, Ph.D.**

Crisp Publications, Inc.
Los Altos, California

RECHARGE YOUR CAREER & YOUR LIFE

by Paul R. Timm, Ph.D.

All rights reserved. No part of this book may be reproduced or transmitted in any form or by any means now known or to be invented, electronic or mechanical, including photocopying, recording, or by any information storage or retrieval system without written permission from the author or publisher, except for the brief inclusion of quotations in a review.

Copyright © 1990 by Paul R. Timm, Ph.D.
Printed in the United States of America

Crisp Publications, Inc.
95 First Street
Los Altos, CA 94022

Library of Congress Catalog Card Number 89-82097
Timm, Paul R. Ph.D.
Recharge Your Career & Your Life
ISBN 1-56052-027-2

CONTENTS

DEDICATION

Life is a marathon, not a sprint. And like any distance runners we sometimes hit "the wall." The ultimate challenge is to push on when the enthusiasm has long faded and the cheers for past accomplishments have become distant memories.

This book is dedicated to my father Roy, my sons Charlie and Jamie, and my brand new grandson, Charles Victor with the hope that we will all live the Bible teaching to "run with patience the race that is set before us."

Paul R. Timm
April 26, 1990

PROLOGUE

Gone are the days when a young person hired on with a company and glided through a career of ever-increasing responsibility, prestige, and earnings to a gold watch retirement 40 years later.

Today, we all face career setbacks and slumps. Some of these result from the changed expectations of worklife. Others stem from an increased willingness to try something new, despite the very real possibility that we may fail. Other setbacks derive from the changing corporate environment that makes even the most secure employers subject to dramatic change. In the past four years, 56 percent of the "Fortune 500" companies have initiated or completed major reorganizations that have dramatically affected their employees. The "secure" has become more fiction than fact.

Just how can we cope with—and overcome—career setbacks and slumps? This book points the way. But first, let's look at three stories that may ring a bell with you. The names are fictitious but the situations are real.

THE CHANDLER'S CHALLENGE

Bill and Linda Chandler seemed to be a storybook couple. He was a pretty fair running back on the high school football team, she, a bubbly blonde cheerleader. Besides being athletic, they were good students— the kind of kids everyone assumed "most likely to succeed."

Both had completed one year at a community college when they decided to get married in the little church on the edge of town. Their new life together seemed assured of happiness; the world lay at their feet. Although their goals were vague, their dreams were sweet, and they believed that they could do anything they wanted to do.

The Chandlers' life together started out being all that they'd hoped for. Their love was strong, and the opportunities for young people in their town were abundant. The largest employer in the county was hiring people at good salaries, and both Bill and Linda took jobs in a manufacturing plant. The work was boring, but the pay and benefits were good. Together, they made more money than either of their dads had made. And they were spending it, too.

Two new cars, a house full of furniture, and some very nice toys were all readily available for easy monthly payments. Shopping became a passion. Linda joked about being inducted into the MasterCard Hall of Fame. The Chandlers' friends envied their prosperity, and life seemed good, indeed.

The honeymoon started to fade when the Chandlers' expenses caught up with, and then passed, their income. Paychecks weren't as exciting now, since they were already spent. Then Mother Nature did her thing, and a new generation of Chandlers was on its way.

The carefree good life suddenly became complicated. Bill started thinking seriously about his responsibilities as a father, and Linda worried about the economic impact of the impending blessed event. To further complicate matters, the plant began laying off people periodically as demand for their products slackened. The competition, it seemed, was building a slightly better mousetrap, and people half a world away were taking jobs from people like Bill and Linda.

The Chandlers began to think long and hard about the realities of life. Both decided that they should have stayed in school and prepared for a profession. Bill really wanted to be an architect like his uncle in Chicago; Linda was fascinated with computers and had an unusual facility for grasping computer languages—at least it seemed so when she'd taken a few programming courses. She felt that her computer savvy and naturally outgoing personality would make her a natural to teach people to use computers. However, the allure of income afforded by working at the plant had deflected them from their career aspirations.

The Chandlers' lives seemed even less fulfilling as they watched high school friends who had gone on to college move up the ladder in their professions. Tom, Dick, and Mary more and more looked like characters on *L.A. Law* as they progressed along their professional fast tracks.

But hey, Bill and Linda were still young. Why not get some additional training and chase their dreams? Bill enrolled in night classes, but Linda stayed home with the baby.

Night after night, Bill plugged along, taking the general courses he needed before he could enroll in the architectural program at the university. But it was a grind. And the costs were high.

Bill and Linda both had a tough time adjusting to the fact that they could no longer buy everything they wanted. Their "dream house" on Elm Street came on the market just when tuition was due and the MasterCard had reached its sizeable limit. Then Linda got laid off from the plant, and the whole load fell on Bill.

About this time, Linda was approached by a neighbor, Sarah, who sold vitamins and food supplements to people in the community. She was doing pretty well in what she called a "multi-level" sales organization, and she explained that her customers said they felt healthier and more vigorous than ever. Sarah asked Linda if she'd like to work for her selling the vitamin and food supplement product line and invited Linda to attend a "rally" promoting her company's joys and opportunities.

What a rally it was! Linda hadn't felt so enthusiastic about anything in years. Why, by building her own sales team, she could make a small fortune working just part time. It seemed the perfect solution.

Eventually, Bill saw the light, too. He quit night school and helped Linda recruit a team of salespeople. The products seemed good, and he felt comfortable selling them, but the big money was in the overrides—the commissions they made on their sales reps' sales. The dream lived on! The Chandlers were going to be wealthy and happy again. The roller coaster was speeding smoothly along, and the wind felt good against their faces.

Then the ride came to a screeching halt. The Food and Drug Administration shut down the company. The vitamins did not meet legal standards; Bill and Linda's multi-level marketing career was over.

Very late one evening, Bill sat at the kitchen table trying to decide which bills to pay and which to string out a little longer. Giving up, he pushed aside the stack of bills, dropped his pen, and rested his head on his arms. "What has happened to us?" he wondered. "Is this what we have to face the rest of our lives?" The old Peggy Lee song, *Is That All There Is?* came to mind, and he began singing it softly as he opened the refrigerator for another beer.

Linda wasn't doing very well, either. She found herself spending more and more time watching soap operas, changing diapers, and eating junk food. She no longer looked like the cheerleader Bill had married; there wasn't much cheer left in her.

The old dreams died that night. There would be no architect or computer trainer in this family. And there was precious little joy. There would be no financial security, and, eventually, there would be no family at all.

The years passed, and the high school sweethearts deemed most likely to succeed lived lives of quiet depression. Occasionally things looked up, but ultimately nothing improved much. The newlyweds' promises and dreams had long ago evaporated, as had their love for each other and their vitality.

What had gone wrong?

FRANK'S MID-LIFE MUDDLE

Funny how people often see themselves very differently from the way others see them. The neighbors all thought Frank Baker a tremendously successful man. He and his wife, Donna, lived in a comfortable home in an upper-middle-class neighborhood. Frank taught at the state university, while Donna worked as a legal assistant for one of the town's better law firms.

Frank's resume was impressive. He had earned three college degrees and been a manager in a big corporation before devoting himself to teaching. He wrote articles for professional journals and had co-authored a textbook used in colleges throughout the country. He traveled regularly as a consultant. Frank was in good physical shape and looked every bit the executive.

For 20 years, he and Donna had had a stable marriage. Their three teenage children seemed well adjusted, successful kids. Although they faced the typical teenage problems, they did well in school, had lots of friends, and found time for part-time jobs and sports.

The Bakers looked like a model family: successful parents, well adjusted kids, even a cocker spaniel. What could be a problem for the Bakers?

Frank felt lousy about his life. Although his resume looked good, he took no joy in his accomplishments. It seemed to him that everyone else was doing better than he was; his accomplishments seemed insignificant; life was quickly passing him by, and there seemed little to look forward to. His merry-go-round had stalled.

As Frank seemed to grow more and more depressed, Donna tried to reason with him. She recited all that he had done and what he meant to her and their family. She grieved that the sparkle in his eyes now seldom appeared. Frank had lost his zest for life. As Frank grew aloof and distracted, Donna became increasingly discouraged. Frank would not confide in her. The Bakers' relationship grew strained. It seemed as though Frank wanted to crawl into a hole and be by himself.

Colleagues and students at the university noticed the change, too. Frank seemed apathetic to his students and increasingly critical of his department. He was particularly impatient with committee meetings. Nothing he did seemed to him to have any relevance.

Frank had always been a physical fitness enthusiast but now even that aspect of his life was modified. He had jogged with a colleague for years but now preferred to jog alone. And jog he did. He stepped up his running mileage sharply as though he wanted to punish his body instead of simply exercising it. In the heat of the summer, he ran more than 200 miles in August—about 50 miles more than his typical monthly distance.

Frank was confused. As he jogged, he thought over and over about all the "stupid, worthless things" he had ever done. He repeatedly called himself derogatory names and even entertained the thought of ending his life. The scary part was when he heard himself agree that ending it all would be a good idea.

Of course, none of this made any sense to an outsider at all. To someone on the outside looking in, Frank had the world by the tail. His life was comfortable; he was well regarded professionally; he and Donna had a good income and few debts; his family was doing well. He had achieved all that he had sought. What more could a man ask for?

ANITA'S ANGUISH

Anita Cushman had been an office manager for a medium-sized home builder, Walker Construction Company, for six years before she got the entrepreneurial bug.

She didn't really mind her job, but it seemed to be a dead-ender. Keeping track of the bills, collections, invoices, and all other paperwork was never regarded as a high priority at Walker. Her bosses' first priority was producing as many moderately priced homes as their crews could assemble in record time. The company valued its track record as almost always making its deadlines. If Sam Walker told you you'd be in your new home by Thanksgiving, by golly, you'd be there.

As office manager, Anita had special talents. She seemed especially good at motivating the other office staff. She had learned lots of shortcuts for being efficient and organized. She got a kick out of seeing people take her suggestions and then work more effectively.

In a word, Anita was good at what she did and she was a good teacher. Eventually, she decided to use her special talents to build a small business of her own. Her neighbor Henry Richards was a sales trainer and independent consultant, and she spoke with him about the opportunities in training. He encouraged Anita to give it a try.

Anita launched her own company, *Secretary Trainers, Inc.* (STI) in October. She had worked for months developing a one-day seminar that taught the skills she had learned. She had selected three cities to test market the seminars and collected mailing lists, flipping through telephone book yellow pages for addresses of companies that might want to send their secretaries to her workshop. She designed a mailout advertisement, pasted on the mailing labels, and sent out the first batch.

The results were encouraging. In each of the three cities, enough people signed up to enable her to cover her expenses and make a small profit. The seminars went well. After each session, she made careful note of any mistakes she made, and over the months, she improved both her program and the logistics of registration, conference room scheduling, materials shipping, etc. STI was off and running.

Secretary Trainers, Inc. grew rapidly. It had found a niche in the training industry. Within a year, Anita had hired several other presenters and was scheduling sessions in scores of cities nationwide. It was like a dream. Everything went right.

After two years of running the operation alone, Anita invited a friend to buy into the company as a partner. The friend, Rosanne Jameson, was a successful accountant who, sick of the large corporation rat race, had just left her job with a financial planning organization. Although Anita and Rosanne were very different in temperament and style, they appreciated each other's skills and formed a good alliance.

The business continued to grow nicely, with Rosanne taking over much of the financial planning and accounting. Rosanne was also well connected in the field of training and development. Her acquaintance, Guy Roberts, who owned a training company of similar size but in a different market, had been looking for an acquisition to increase the size of his company. He approached Rosanne and Anita.

He proposed to buy out their company for some cash and significant stock in his company. By increasing the size of the two companies, they could then take the firm public and sell stock to other investors for a big gain. After several months of negotiation, a deal was struck, and Guy paid each of the women $50,000, plus 100,000 shares of stock in his company. He claimed that the stock was worth $8 to $10 per share, although verification was not possible since it could not be sold on the open market.

Several months later, the business slumped. Guy's reaction was to blame STI for the troubles. Despite contracts that assured job security, he fired Anita, retaining Rosanne as president of the division.

Anita was shocked. She had been fired from her own company! She immediately considered taking legal action against Guy but put off doing so because of the high costs of lawyers and court fees. At any rate, she wasn't sure she could win. The contracts were somewhat vague.

The money from the buyout and the stock (which could not be traded until the company was publicly offered) were all she had. She was out. And she was furious.

Her lawyer examined the sale contracts and regretfully informed her that she had been had. Roberts' promise to make a public stock offering was not likely to happen any time soon (if ever). In the meanwhile, Anita found herself facing the prospect of starting over or going back to work for someone else.

Day after day, Anita kicks herself for having been so naive and trusting. Her baby, the company she'd built from scratch, was now beyond her reach. She didn't have the faintest idea what to do next. All she knew for sure was that she hated Guy Roberts and her former friend Rosanne.

Each morning she looks herself in the mirror and says, "Nice going, dummy. Here you are pushing 40, and your career is in shambles. You blew it. You'll never again have a success. You're entirely too stupid to make it in today's business world."

The stories of the Chandlers, Frank, and Anita are dedicated to the ambitious person—like you—who took the roller coaster to the top more than a few times. You experienced the long, slow grind uphill and then the invigorating rush down the other side. You know that the journey to success is a noisy, bumpy one, with frequent twists and turns and that it's guaranteed to blow your hat off.

At times, you exceeded your rosiest predictions and felt invincible. Ah, how sweet those times were! You could do no wrong; nothing could stop you. Your performance got a standing ovation.

But other times, your roller coaster stalled. You felt no enthusiasm and everything went wrong. Applause was a distant memory. All too vivid were feelings of helplessness, disappointment, and fear. Oh yes, you came close, but somewhere along the line the dream had faded and a grim reality had drifted in like fog off the ocean.

This experience is pretty depressing isn't it? It sure was for me! But take consolation in these three facts:

1. **You are not alone** because everyone experiences slumps and setbacks. The precise symptoms may differ, but when you get them, you know it. It's up to you what you do about them.
2. **You can, and will, bounce back** by applying the simple but powerful ideas you'll learn in this book. Not only will you bounce back to "normal," but *you'll advance to greater successes* than you ever dared dream of. I can assure you of this. Certain laws and principles are inevitable. Once you understand and apply them, nothing can stop you from achieving all that you want.
3. **Setbacks are helpful** for we learn much of value from them. By seeing past mistakes or misfortune as part of a learning process, we can actually welcome them. Our personal knowledge is what makes each of us unique and valuable.

INTRODUCTION _____

_____

Welcome to the Slump

The stories recounted have for a common denominator the feelings of failure and crushing disappointment felt by the players, all success-oriented people. They all sought success and, for a time, they experienced it. But their perspective has been foreshortened by THE SLUMP. Day-to-day life is a matter of survival, not growth.

Technically, airplanes are off course 90 percent of the time. But the pilot and on-board computer keep making the little mid-course corrections that ultimately land the plane at its intended destination. This is exactly the case with goal-directed people.

History is replete with losers turned winners. Indeed, every winner has known losses. Lincoln lost more elections than he won, and Babe Ruth struck out many more times than he hit homeruns. Life is inevitably a succession of wins, losses, and a few rain-outs. We all toddle before we walk, walk before we run. And we all fall off the track now and then. We all face THE SLUMP.

Believe me; I've been there. Your slump is different than mine, and it may hit you when you are older or younger than I was, and it may hit at a different stage in your career. No matter. But luckily for you, you'll have a weapon I didn't have: this book.

I promise you that if you'll apply the suggestions in this book, you will not only survive your slump but profit from it. You'll recharge and be better than ever.

But Meanwhile, I'm Depressed

I counseled a man who described his view of the world in this way:

> I usually feel like a kid with my nose pressed against the window, looking in on the party to which I wasn't invited. The goals I've been chasing have turned out to be like soap bubbles; once I get them, they seem empty and meaningless. It seems that I'm forever "oh-so-close" to achieving "THE BIG ONE" (whatever that is at the time), only to see it slip-slidin' away. I feel like the guy who reached for that brass ring just as his horse tripped. I get the feeling that when my ship comes in, I'll be at the airport.

Life doesn't have to be this way for you. Not if you use the bounce-back techniques described in this book, starting with the realization that . . .

We Flop Before We Fly

Every achiever suffers inevitable setbacks. We flop before we fly, and often, we flop again even after we've been flying. Today's career is fraught with uncertainty and constant change, much of which we cannot anticipate or control.

This book teaches what Paul Harvey would call "the rest of the story" about success. It tells you how to bounce back from the inevitable fall. It shows you how to pursue and achieve your goals with confidence. It should inspire you to rediscover your dream for a richer, fuller life. It teaches you what to do for an encore.

How the Book Works

First, the ideas in this book are psychologically sound. They have been proved *effective* by tens of thousands of high achievers who made these tips their *habits* and reaped the rewards.

Og Mandino, author of *The Greatest Secret in the World,* writes that "The only difference between those who have failed and those who have succeeded lies in the differences in their habits. Good habits are the key to all success. Bad habits unlock the door to failure."

Secondly, this book teaches the principle of "superiority of force," which confers an overwhelming advantage over other approaches you may have tried. Superiority of force, a military leader would tell us, implies a multi-dimensional attack. We attack the forces that destroy our dreams, overcoming discouragement, apathy, a sense of failure.

The third way this book works is by teaching you the power of multipliers that produce quantum jumps forward.

Principle #1: Getting Back to the Basics

Bounce-back habits are simple and rooted in what athletic coaches call "the fundamentals." Vince Lombardi, the legendary coach of the Green Bay Packers during their glory years, was getting exasperated by his team's poor play during the first half of a game. At half time, he gathered his team in the locker room and preached his favorite theme: "Football success is a matter of solid fundamentals." When he had the players' attention, he held up a football and said, "Gentlemen, it's time to get back to basics. This is a football."

One lineman asked, "Can you go over that a little slower, coach?" but the rest of the team got the message. When the game isn't going the way you'd like—if life isn't giving you what you want—the best way to fix it is by *going back to the basics.*

Blocking and tackling, passing and catching are the basics of football, and Pro-Bowl players practice them constantly. For basketball players, constant practice at shooting and ball handling is the only path to the NBA. Top pro golfers are never completely satisfied with their swing; when they slump, they concentrate on their swing. Similarly, professional writers constantly look for that perfect phrase. Top systems analysts are ever vigilant for the most elegant, effective programming solutions. Pianists practice scales. Mastery of basic techniques is fundamental to peak performance for all, no matter what their profession.

This is a block-and-tackle book. But don't be mislead by the notion that the ideas presented here are too simple to be effective. Quite the contrary. Simple techniques, faithfully and consistently applied, are the most powerful of all in advancing you toward your goals.

Principle #2: The Superiority of Force

In addition to making habitual basic techniques, we court success by using the military principle superiority of force. The great military strategists use this approach to overwhelm an enemy. The enemy who cannot be beaten by a division of infantry can surely be defeated by a combination of infantry, armor, artillery, and air strikes. The good news is that we have five major weapons, or power sources, that assure us superiority of force. These weapons take the form of simple statements, none more than four words. All five together total only 15 words. But as a formula for success and rebounding from setbacks, they comprise the FIVE BEST IDEAS ever. This is not solely my opinion; I have lots of company in this belief. Virtually every psychologist will agree with me, although each may phrase the ideas differently. Psychologists often use bigger words, but I like to keep things simple. Here they are:

THE FIVE BEST IDEAS EVER FOR ACHIEVING SUCCESS

1. **LIKE YOURSELF**
2. **DO THE RIGHT THINGS**
3. **DO THINGS RIGHT**
4. **TREAT OTHERS WELL**
5. **STICK WITH IT**

Nothing too complicated there. You don't have to be a brain surgeon to apply these ideas. With a little guidance, anyone can practice them. Like many simple things, these ideas are exceptionally powerful.

With these five weapons, the enemy doesn't stand a chance! But let me caution you. The key to winning this battle lies in mastering *all five* simultaneously. They work together. Too often people teach us their favorite weapon. But if a soldier has only one weapon, and that weapon misfires, he's in big trouble. Using superiority of forces means using everything in the arsenal.

Each of us has a different level of skill in applying success principles. Books or tapes that teach just one principle can fall short. Sometimes the success tips we've tried in the past simply don't work for us or won't work at a particular moment. Another weapon is needed. Life doesn't always hit us with just one obstacle at a time. It has been said that Custer could have become one of our nation's most famous heroes if he could have gotten the Sioux to attack over the hill one at a time.

Principle #3: The Quantum Jumps

When basic habits and the five best ideas are used in tandem, the result is quantum jumps in personal effectiveness.

I strongly believe in quantum jumps—those leaps from the status quo to undreamed-of levels of accomplishment. I've seen them in my life, and so will you.

For example, in 1986 I made about the same amount of money that I did in 1985. For that matter, it was about the same as in 1984, 1983, and the previous several years. True, there was a small growth in my income but, when adjusted for inflation, my rewards were pretty flat. I was doing okay. In fact, my income probably placed me among the top 10 or 15 percent of wage earners in my state. I was comfortable but not affluent.

Then I decided to go to war against stagnation and apathy. I was sick of a no-growth personal economy. I had long been a believer in the possibility of major jumps forward. They'd occurred in other areas of my life, so I figured, "Why not with my income?"

Just a few years earlier, I had made such a jump in my jogging mileage. I had kept track of my running distance for years; it didn't vary much. Then I changed my mindset, circumstances, attitudes, and behaviors. I started running with another fellow. We adjusted the time of day we ran, so we wouldn't be delayed by other commitments. We set goals and actually started enjoying the runs.

We also looked at our jogging routine as a multiplier, using the exercise time for several worthwhile purposes. We multiplied our benefits by talking, planning, and discussing ideas while running. We met needs for enlightenment, socializing, problem solving, and comraderie while we promoted physical fitness. Result: our running mileage more than doubled, and it's doubled again since. Instead of jogging 300-400 miles a year, we found that we'd run 1000 miles—our first goal. The next year we ran 1200 miles. Then 1500. Then 1800. The longer distances became habitual, and my health and physical vitality have never been better.

Likewise, in 1987 I applied the simple techniques I'll show you in this book to jump from a top-15-percent wage earner to a top *one* percent wage earner. My income more than doubled, and I know that it'll keep climbing as long as I persist in using the techniques in this book (or until my financial goals are no longer important to me).

The premise of this book is that quantum jumps in success in any area come about when we apply the five best ideas on a sustained basis until they become habits.

Just as Chinese water torture plinks away on its victim to devastating effect, the same water can create a magnificent canyon. Likewise, constant application of the five power sources in this book will inevitably bring about dramatic results.

So let's forget the stumbles, miscues, and crummy deals of the past. The past is beyond our control, so forget it. Lousy things have happened to everybody. The difference between winners and losers lies in how they bounce back.

BEST IDEA 1

Like Yourself

ARNULFO L. OLIVEIRA MEMORIAL LIBRARY
1825 MAY STREET
BROWNSVILLE, TEXAS 78520

CHAPTER 1

REBUILD YOUR SELF-CONFIDENCE _____

> *Remember, happiness doesn't depend upon who you are or what you have; it depends solely upon what you think.*
>
> —Dale Carnegie

> *No one can make you feel inferior without your consent.*
>
> —Eleanor Roosevelt

The Philadelphia Eagles football team was having a bad year. In a town notorious for abusive fans (someone once quipped, "They'd boo a cure for cancer"), quarterback Ron Jaworski was the lightning rod for the crowd's frustration. One Sunday, a large, hand-painted sheet was draped from the stands. The TV cameras focused on it several times during the game. On it was scrawled these words of encouragement: "Don't worry, Ron. We still love you—Mom and Dad." But "Dad" was crossed out. How's that for a confidence builder?

What happened to me received little publicity, but it made me feel terrible. It was several years ago now, but it's still vivid in my mind. I can remember the day, the hour, the moment.

No monumental disaster was its cause. No, it was more an accumulation of little, irritating setbacks that finally found me sitting in my favorite chair, staring into space. I recited all the stupid things I'd done. The opportunities lost, the promising business opportunities that suddenly turned to dirt, the long stream of miscues all haunted me. I was almost paralyzed; I sat there wallowing in my self-disgust.

After what seemed like hours of rehearsing my shortcomings and lamenting the unfairness of it all, I decided to get up and go to the golf driving range. Maybe I could pound a few dozen golf balls into oblivion and take my mind off my troubles.

I dragged my seldom-used clubs out of the garage and drove to the range. It was a sunny May afternoon, but that didn't help my disposition. "Gimme a bucket of balls," I growled at the kid in the pro shop. "I'm sorry, sir," he replied somewhat sheepishly, "the driving range is closed." "Closed?" I bellowed. "Why the hell would the driving range be closed on a sunny afternoon like this?"

"We're out of balls," the kid stammered. "The tractor that picks 'em up ran out of gas, and I can't get away from the shop to go get more gas, and, besides, there's nobody here to drive the tractor. . . ." He rambled on, but I'd tuned him out by then.

"Out of balls." That seemed to sum up my life in general. All the balls—all the good things in life—had already been played by the guy who got there before the tractor ran out of gas. I started to see myself as the old Al Capp cartoon character with the dark cloud hanging over his head.

I returned home and plopped down in my chair. Nothing was working for me. My self-concept couldn't have been any lower. The world seemed to have turned against me. I wanted to scream!

Then it happened. A small voice deep within became barely audible. It was repeating lines from some of those self-help tapes I'd listened to back in the old days when I was successful: My subconscious seemed to be on one of its "search and annoy" missions. I couldn't tune it out. It said, "Get a hold of yourself." It said, "Only you can create your own happiness." It said, "Haven't you had enough self-pity for now? Isn't it time to turn things around?" The cliches were driving me crazy!

Then it said in a more straightforward manner, "Quit being a jerk." (The still, small voice was getting impatient!) This scored a direct hit. Like a whiff of smelling salts, these words snapped my mind back to alertness. It was true: I *was* being a jerk.

I determined then that it was time to get a hold of my mind and my attitudes. Why was I flogging myself? Sure, I'd made mistakes, and circumstances had worked against me, but that happens to everybody. Why not think about the positive things in life. There were still lots of good things in life. But first, I had to lift this cloud of gloom and self-pity. I reminded myself that everybody has setbacks and the difference between winners and losers lay in how many times they get back up. It was time for me to practice some of what I'd preached. It was time to recharge.

This was a turning point: I decided to take charge of my life and make things happen, not simply float along as a victim of circumstance. It was literally the very next day when several major opportunities came my way, one of them resulting in a quantum leap in my career and immediate earnings. Of course, the process of bouncing back doesn't always happen so quickly. But it will happen for you if you let it.

Please don't get the idea from this that I have never been down again since. I, like you, have mood swings and low periods in my life. That dreaded monster, THE SLUMP, rears its ugly head every now and then. Sometimes, he moves in with me for a few weeks like a relentless in-law. But I've learned how to evict him by applying the techniques in this book.

TRY THIS: Sit back, relax, and close your eyes. Now recreate in your mind the moment you "hit bottom." Recall in the most vivid detail possible the feelings, images, sounds, and smells associated with that experience. Jot down a description of the circumstances in this box.

Now close your eyes again and change the focus in your mind. Picture the feelings you had then as fading away, as becoming dull and dark. Distort the mental picture, force it out of focus, and imagine that it is fading into a dark hole in space. Soon the experience will no longer exist for you. It's gone.

Your #1 Power Source or Power Drain

More than brainpower, ambition, or talent, self-confidence enables us to bounce back from any setback—and give a great encore. Confidence is our power source for directing and changing our world. When we have self-confidence, we trust ourselves to make decisions, formulate plans, and make good things happen. Without sufficient self-esteem, we can accomplish little of value.

In the war against setbacks and slumps, self-esteem is often the first casualty. We feel embarrassed, discouraged, outraged, and frustrated. To some extent, high achievers, who take personal responsibility for their lives, blame themselves. This in itself is normal and can be a healthy reaction.

What Is Self-Confidence?

Self-confidence has many names: self-worth, self-esteem, self-respect. I use them interchangeably, although there are subtle differences. All these terms describe a basic, healthy belief in, and love of, self. Such self-love enables us to say,

- I am a valuable person.
- My opinions and thoughts are worthwhile.
- I can accomplish great things.
- I deserve to be successful. And most important,
- I like and respect myself.

It is self-appreciation and self-love that enables successful people to recognize and use their talents and abilities. The trick to developing or restoring positive self-esteem lies in filling and regularly replenishing our "love basket." Picture a picnic basket full of good food. These goodies represent self-love. If the food is bad or the basket empty, we're in serious trouble. We need to stop at the market and stock up on the freshest and most delicious food.

Grab the Handle of Your Love Basket

Picture yourself carrying a picnic basket. This basket contains the nourishment for your psychological self. For some people, the basket's nourishment is the kind that builds a strong psyche—health food for the mind. For others, the basket holds junk food—processed munchies with empty calories. Usually we pack our own basket, although other people can contribute a "treat" for us, too.

The health food basket provides a true and *authentic love* supply; the junk food basket provides *cheap love substitutes*.

Authentic Self-Love

Authentic love (health food for the mind) is *unconditional.* It nourishes us with the knowledge that we are loved *regardless of the mistakes we make or the setbacks we encounter.* It says that we are of great value; we are prized and treasured for all that we are or may become. There are *no strings attached* to authentic love. This love recognizes that we are human—we make mistakes, we misjudge, we get into bad situations. So what? That's what humans do! Accept that—and *forgive yourself.*

When other people help you pack your authentic basket, the love expressed means:

- I trust you; you are worthy of trust.
- I have confidence and faith in you; you can do it.
- I admire and prize you; you are of great worth.
- I'm with you win, lose, or draw; it makes no difference.
- This love is truth and not a false substitute.

Love Substitutes

The junk food basket carries cheap love substitutes. This kind of love is *conditional;* it comes with many strings attached. It tends to be *tied to behavior and external appearance.* Self-love substitutes don't let us acknowledge our humanity. They sharply limit the mistakes we can make. If we exceed the limit, we are deemed unworthy.

When other people stock our basket with junk food or when we choose to accept love substitutes, we hear statements like these:

- I love you when you look good, when you're pretty or handsome.
- I love you when you do what I want.
- I love you as long as you don't make mistakes. Blow this one and we're finished.
- I love you when you're a winner; losers don't deserve my love.

This type of "love" is artificial and fleeting. It has no lasting value and rings hollow.

Which basket do you want to carry? Obviously, one is far better for you than the other, yet many people choose love substitutes. They feed themselves junk food and never enjoy the great feeling that accompanies unconditional acceptance and love.

> **TRY THIS:**   Picture your love basket. What is in it now? Describe the love substitutes and the authentic "foodstuffs." Do you come up short in real nourishment?

We constantly refill our love basket, and what we fill it with is largely up to us. Garbage in our basket tends to attract more garbage; healthy thoughts attract more of the same. This "law of attraction" works every time. We really do attract to ourselves thoughts, people, and circumstances that coincide with our self-concept. We get all that we feel we deserve; no more, no less.

People with healthy self-esteem know that they deserve all the good things that life offers. People whose baskets are full of love substitutes attract success substitutes—conditional approval that evaporates when they stumble.

Love substitutes remind me of the story of the fellow who tried to catch mice by putting a picture of a piece of cheese in the mousetrap. He caught a picture of a mouse. Nothing real or lasting can come from a self-concept built on love substitutes.

Getting Our Minimum Daily Requirement of Strokes

While our innate sense of self-love forms a foundation for high self-esteem, we still need reinforcement from others. After all, we are social animals and we value others' opinions and responses.

Just as our body has a minimum daily requirement (MDR) of vitamins and nutrients, our psychological side has an MDR for positive "strokes."

A "stroke" is simply a unit of recognition—usually a compliment or comment from others that means, "I value you." Positive stroking can range from a smile or a wink to a detailed expression of affection. It enhances and builds our confidence.

Negative stroking (anything from a frown to blistering criticism) can diminish us or make us question our self-worth.

Normally, we think of stroking as coming from others, but we can also boost our self-confidence from self-recognition. Indeed, for most well-adjusted people, internally generated strokes are the most valued and powerful sources of nourishment for our egos.

But regardless of the source of our positive strokes, we must get our MDR of high-quality strokes in order to function and to grow.

> Everyone walks around with an invisible neon sign on his or her forehead that says: MAKE ME FEEL IMPORTANT.

The lack of positive strokes prompts us to underrate and undervalue ourselves. This underrating becomes a self-perpetuating cycle. The less we value and believe in ourselves, the more we invite others to think less of us and treat us poorly. The bad news is that we invite negative stroking when we are down on ourselves. This becomes a negative, self-defeating cycle. The good news is that we can control the kind and amount of positive strokes we receive from ourselves and others. We thus ensure ourselves a steady supply of confidence builders. More on how to do this later, but first . . .

TRY THIS: **How's Your Self-Esteem Now?**

Take a moment to answer the self-evaluation on page 24 to assess your level of self-confidence. Use a simple 1-5 scale to determine how strongly you agree or disagree with each statement in the quiz.

1. means you *strongly disagree* with the statement
2. means you *disagree*
3. means you neither agree nor disagree—*you are neutral* or *undecided*
4. means you *agree*
5. means you *strongly agree* with the statement

	Score
1. I would rather be me than anyone else.	_____
2. I can handle difficult situations effectively.	_____
3. I enjoy my own company.	_____
4. I am a successful person.	_____
5. I rarely make serious mistakes.	_____
6. Other people like to be with me.	_____
7. I make good judgement calls.	_____
8. Other people listen to my ideas.	_____
9. I am competent.	_____
10. I have lots of good ideas.	_____
11. It's easy for me to make friends.	_____
12. It's easy for me to attract the opposite sex.	_____
13. In social groups, people seek my company.	_____
14. When I look in a mirror, I like what I see.	_____
15. I like myself.	_____
Total Score	_____

The maximum possible score is 75. There are, of course, no right or wrong answers, nor is there a typical score. But the object of the game would be to score as high as possible. If your score isn't what you want it to be, you can take charge of changing it. In the remainder of this chapter we will look at typical barriers to high self-esteem and ways to overcome them. By applying the tips provided on a regular basis, you will learn once again to like yourself.

The Insidious Nature of Negative Strokes

Even if you pride yourself on being tough-minded and thick-skinned, you may be getting zinged by negative strokes more than you realize.

Little things can nibble away at your esteem more than the big things. Mother Nature protects the largest, strongest beast in the jungle with a thick hide, yet many an elephant has suffered a painful death when insects crawled into its ear, multiplied, and destroyed its brain.

And while I'm using jungle metaphors, consider how many people you know who have been bitten by a rhinoceros, hippo, or even a lion. Do you know anyone personally? I don't either. But I know lots of people who have been bitten by mosquitos, gnats, or horseflies. It's not the big bites that chew away our self-confidence, it's the little, irritating stings. Frequent negative strokes, minor criticisms and complaints, are discouraging: mosquito bites to our self-esteem can leave scars.

But keep one important fact in mind. We can fend off or throw out negative thoughts—the junk food that gets into our basket. With mental discipline, we can accept or reject strokes. We own our own thoughts, which we can digest or throw away. Talk to yourself about renegade negative thoughts and run them off by crowding them out with positive self-talk. (More on this later.)

We inevitably seem to recall more negative than positive strokes. There are lots of bugs out there and our cologne seems to attract them. But once we become aware of where these bugs are nesting, we can eradicate them before they bite.

Five common situations cause us to focus on negatives while craving positive strokes:

1. The 80/20 Reversal (or the Case of the Missing Compliment)

At least 80 percent of the time people close to you think you're terrific. They admire many things about you. They like your appearance, your talents, abilities, your personality in general. They also assume you know how they feel, so why should they bother to mention it?

About 20 percent of the time they notice ways in which they think you could improve. These things they are quick to point out. After all, you must not know these things about yourself or you would already have changed, right? So here comes a swarm of "helpful" gnats.

A reason for the 80/20 reversal is that our faults can be inconvenient and irritating to others while our strengths are not. People are always more inclined to mention what bothers them than what favorably impresses them.

Another reason that compliments often are not expressed is that our friends fear that we will become conceited if we're over-stroked. So rather than overload our basket with praise, they keep our self-esteem on a diet.

Rhonda was the lovely daughter of two devoted, if somewhat rigid, parents. She was their proverbial pride and joy. Her parents were determined to help her "make something of herself." They seemed to overlook the fact that she already *is* something (unconditional love), and she received the impression that the current Rhonda wasn't quite good enough (love substitutes).

When as a teenager Rhonda brought home a "B" average report card, her parents insisted that she could do better. When she came home with an "A" report card, they said it was "about time." They proceeded to "help" her by lecturing and moralizing. When she excelled, they smiled proudly, but secretly, to themselves. They didn't want her to get a big head.

As Rhonda grew to adulthood, she became increasingly resentful toward her parents whose life goal *seemed* to be pointing out her imperfections. But more than that, Rhonda became an insecure woman who felt that she could never achieve anything important. Because she seldom received her minimum daily requirement of positive stroking, she was unable to develop a basic love of self. Her parents were baffled by her constant self-doubt and shocked by her resentment toward them. They had helped fill her love basket with the junk food of *conditional* love.

As a result of the 80/20 reversal, you, like Rhonda, can plan on hearing about eight criticisms for *every* two compliments. What you really deserve is just the opposite, but life isn't fair. So don't depend totally on the strokes other people may or may not provide. Learn to get your strokes somewhere else—from your own love basket, for example.

> **TRY THIS:**   Plant the following idea in your mind: Every complaint we hear means there have been at least four unspoken compliments. Negative strokes should remind us of these unspoken positives. Write this idea in your own words in this box.
>
>
>
> We must make the effort to give our "positives" equal time on the television of our mind.

2. The Misdirected Negative (or Wearing a Magnetic Flak Jacket)

Some people seem to attract negative comments. They take any negative comments personally, even those not directed at them. They seem to suck in overheard remarks and criticisms and assume they apply to them. Like the old Laugh-In television skit, they repeatedly ask people to "sock it to me," even when they are not the target.

Freddy, the personnel manager of a savings and loan, had been on a diet for several weeks and had lost 10 pounds. With about 10 more still to lose, Freddy's willpower deserted him one morning when the snack cart came around. He ate two chocolate doughnuts. At noon, he went to lunch with three of his co-workers. After he had ordered a light meal, he went to the men's room. As he returned to the table, he overheard Susan saying, "Anyone who eats doughnuts at morning break is bound to be a blimp." Freddy rejoined the group at the table with a weak smile and sat without speaking through the meal. He was silently smoldering.

The reality was that no one knew that Freddy had eaten doughnuts that morning. Susan had directed her comment at herself for the two doughnuts *she* had eaten at morning break. In fact, she had noticed that Freddy was looking slimmer (but the 80/20 reversal caused her to fail to mention it), and she was disappointed in herself for not doing as well.

Don't assume that you are the target of overheard remarks. Don't insist on turning a verbal gun upon yourself. You'll end up shooting holes in your love basket.

TRY THIS: Describe an example where you may have caught a misdirected negative.

---

3. The Jealous Negative (If I Can't Keep Up, Shoot the Competition)

Sometimes, people try to make themselves feel better by criticizing others. Even trivial wounding comments can poke holes in our love basket. Janet's story typifies this:

Janet was a new first grade school teacher in her early twenties. She was an attractive, enthusiastic person who was anxious to learn from the more experienced first grade teacher, Sybil. One afternoon, as the two women planned lessons together, the veteran teacher tilted her head to one side and squinted at Janet for a moment. She then said, "Have you ever noticed that your left eyelid droops?"

Janet was stunned by the remark. She laughed it off at the time, but when she got home, she went straight to the mirror to study her reflection. To her horror, she discovered that it *did* droop slightly.

For several days she felt that everyone who looked at her was thinking about her "deformed" eyelid. "Old droopy eye," they'd no doubt call her. She thought about making an appointment with a plastic surgeon to have the gross deformity repaired.

She asked her husband if he had ever noticed that her eyelid drooped. He hadn't. She called her mother long distance to ask her how serious she thought the problem was. Her mother had never noticed it either. Janet finally decided that the problem must not be too serious. She learned to ignore it most of the time, but she still thought about it now and then when she looked in the mirror.

In reality, Sybil was simply jealous of Janet. She felt that Janet was more attractive and talented than she was. Sybil thought she might feel better about herself if she found things about Janet to criticize. It didn't work, though. It never does. Sybil succeeded in making Janet feel bad, but she failed to feel any better herself.

Recognize the jealous negative as a left-handed compliment. You must be pretty sharp if others feel threatened by you.

> **TRY THIS:** Describe an example where a negative stroke you received may have been a result of jealousy. Restate that comment to express the real feelings underlying it. What did the person really mean?

4. The Inaccurate Negative (Kick-the-Dog Syndrome)

Sometimes you may be blasted by a negative comment that doesn't seem to have anything to do with you but simply releases tension for the sender of the message. A television commercial for aspirin showed a person who had been yelled at saying, "Sure, you've got a headache, but don't take it out on me."

Sometimes you receive the brunt of a blast of negatives because you were at the wrong place at the wrong time, not because you deserve criticism.

In such cases, it is important to remember that you don't have to accept everything people want to put in your basket. Learn to recognize when others are just blowing off steam.

> **TRY THIS:** Describe an example where you received (or gave) a negative stroke that was really just a release of frustration.

5. The Silent Treatment (No News is Definitely *Not* Good News)

If we receive neither positive nor negative strokes from other people, most of us assume that we are simply "just okay" or that we are not liked and/or respected. Neither of these messages replenishes the basket. No news is definitely not good news when it comes to self-confidence.

Our need for stroking is particularly frustrated when we receive *no* strokes. For many people, that's even worse than receiving a negative stroke. The cruelest thing we can do to a fellow human is to ignore him or her totally.

An old Carol Burnett TV skit comes to mind. Carol is in a restaurant with her date, played by the handsome Lyle Wagoner. The premise of the skit is that Carol will be ignored totally—treated as though invisible. The waitress takes Lyle's order, looks right past Carol, and walks away. Carol's character tries to get the waitress's attention, but to no avail. As the skit develops, Carol's behavior becomes more bizarre. She does everything possible to get the attention of someone—anyone! Ultimately, she is seen clinging to the ankle of a man, still oblivious to her existence, as he drags her from the restaurant! Nothing is more damaging to a person's sense of self than to be ignored.

The behavior of young children is highly instructive in this matter. Kids simply refuse to be ignored, as all parents know. Mom is taking a long telephone call and consequently ignoring her toddler. At first, baby may entertain herself, but when her need for stroking becomes too great, she *demands* attention. If cute antics don't get mom's attention, obnoxious ones will. A bowl of cereal dumped over mom's head will surely merit some attention, even if it's negative.

Most adults will resort to some equivalent of dumping cereal if, as a result of the silent treatment, we become sufficiently starved for strokes.

Receiving strokes from others is one way for us to replenish our love basket, but it's not the only way. We have far more control over *internal* sources of nourishment. Don't assume that no news is bad news; expect the opposite.

> **TRY THIS:** Describe an experience where you assumed no answer was a negative when in reality it was positive.

6. Especially for Women (Guys, you can read this too)

Everyone faces the challenge of securing that MDR of strokes. Women, however, often face additional barriers that can become confidence crushers.

Many women feel that, historically, women have been undervalued in our culture and are still seriously underrated. After all, if women can't "tote that barge and lift that bale," how useful can they be? Societies are slow to change. Logically, everyone knows that an inability to bench press 200 pounds has nothing to do with mental prowess, but some people still behave as though it does. Decisions made in board rooms often require effective mental arm wrestling but rarely do elbows really hit the table. Women can be subtly conditioned by society to feel as if they are less capable than men. As a result, they undervalue both their own efforts and those of other women.

Many women think they have fewer opportunities for self-discovery than men typically have. They describe themselves in terms of others, and their successes depend on the successes of others. Their self-esteem may be hitched totally to their husband's or children's accomplishments. When asked who she is, a woman may respond, "I'm the wife of George Smith, the attorney," or "I'm the mother of Betty Brown, the track star." But who, exactly, is *she?*

In other cases, women see themselves as good wives, mothers, and caring and unselfish people. They see themselves as everything society says a good woman should be. Nevertheless, they don't feel content with such label descriptions, because the qualities associated with being a good woman (e.g., emotionality, sensitivity, compassion, cooperativeness) have not traditionally been as highly regarded as those associated with being a successful man (e.g., strength, decisiveness, independence, leadership ability).

Consequently, women who have worked hard to live up to cultural expectations may also have learned to devalue the very traits to which they have aspired. They tend to say, "I'm *only* a mother and homemaker" or I'm *only* a secretary."

Too many women subscribe to the notion that *if I'm good at it, it really can't matter much.* The woman who says, "Oh sure, I'm usually patient with the kids, and I'm a good cook, but I need to lose 10 pounds and I'm not as lively as I used to be," can't put into perspective the normal balance between successes and shortcomings common to us all. She permits her imperfections to overwhelm her winning characteristics until the things she's good at have no value in her eyes.

Women are more likely than men to depreciate themselves. Asked to describe themselves, many women immediately launch a string of negatives. "Well," a woman might say, "I'm not particularly good looking, and I'm a little overweight, and I'm not good at sports, and I'm not as much fun to be around as Nancy, and I'm not as intelligent as my husband..."

Such women tend to have impossibly high standards for themselves. They not only want to be "perfect," but they want to be perfect in *everything* they do. For such women, self-assessment is an all-or-nothing game. If they aren't beautiful, they're ugly; if they're not as thin as a model, they're slobs; if they aren't geniuses, they're dumb.

Finally, many women today suffer in self-esteem because they are understandably confused about the expectations of modern life. Everyone wrestles with the age-old question "What is the meaning of life?" but for women of the 1990s that question has become particularly difficult to answer. Regardless of what she devotes herself to—career, family, husband, parents, church work, etc., one day she inevitably asks, "Is this all there is?"

To this question there is no easy answer, but much promise can be found in seeking a balance in our daily activities and life goals. (I'll discuss this in the remainder of the book, beginning in Chapter 2.)

TRY THIS: Make two lists. In the left column, list what you think "the world" expects of you. In the right column, describe what you expect from others. Use this list as a basis for a discussion with your spouse or partner. What discrepancies need to be reconciled?

How "The Way We Word" Affects Self-Esteem

How we use language to describe the world around us has a lot to do with our self-esteem. Studies show that people with low self-esteem tend to see the world in terms of black and white, good and bad, right and wrong. Everything is one extreme or the other. People with stronger self-concepts view the world in terms of shades of gray, as mixtures of good and bad.

If someone were to ask you if you are a good person or a bad person, how would you respond? If asked if you are rich or poor? If asked if you are big or little? Some people would respond quickly with one word or the other. Others might ask, "Compared to what?"

As small children, we learn about absolutes. As adults, we need to experience reality in a comparative way. It's enough for a child to know that the stove is "hot" to avoid being burned. As adults, it's important to understand that heat is a matter of degree: 325° F is fine for baking cookies, 400° F for baking potatoes, and "broil" the best for cooking steak.

TRY THIS:

Place a check mark next to the adjective in each pair that describes you:

☐	tall	☐	short
☐	rich	☐	poor
☐	smart	☐	stupid
☐	successful	☐	failure
☐	good	☐	bad
☐	fat	☐	thin
☐	beautiful	☐	ugly
☐	strong	☐	weak
☐	competent	☐	inept

Were you uncomfortable with these limited choices? Do you think these terms describe you accurately? Of course they don't. They are absolutes, and there are precious few absolutes in this world.

But when we start to label people, including ourselves, we are using an overly simplistic and unproductive way of thinking. In short, we are filling our love basket with junk. The words we use force us into unrealistic descriptions. We then react to these descriptions as if they were real.

The good news is that by becoming aware of such pernicious either-or thinking, we can change. By adjusting our language, we change our world.

TRY THIS:

It is useful to regard the world as a forest of measuring sticks or scales. These scales allow us to see ourselves in relative terms. For example, place an X somewhere on the line between each set of adjectives below to show where you rate yourself *compared to people with whom you associate:*

rich —————————————	poor
fat —————————————————	thin
successful —————————	failure
strong ——————————————	weak
disciplined ———————	undisciplined
smart ———————————	stupid
skilled —————————	unskilled

You may still feel uncomfortable about rating yourself on such a scale, but at least you have more than two choices and can compare yourself with specific others, your associates. This allows *relative* rather than *absolute* judgements and a more accurate assessment of reality.

We can think of life as having thousands of these scales upon which we rate ourselves constantly. For example, if you were asked where you'd rate your appearance on a 10 point scale, you might say, "Oh, I'm about a seven."

Great, but are you also a "seven" in your ability to repair things around the house? How about your skills at dealing with sales people? How about your penmanship? How about your ability to help your children with homework? How about your ability to handle finances? The list is endless and so are the possible ratings. On some, we score pretty high, on others, lower. This makes up our unique character. There has never been and will never be another you or me. God threw away the mold.

The scales are themselves relative. I once overheard a person interviewing a potential employee. The interviewer inquired, "Nancy, tell me about your greatest strengths."

"Well, I'm a good secretary," she replied.

"Really, how good?"

"I can type 75 to 80 words a minute, and I make only two or three mistakes on a typical typing test."

The interviewer responded, "That's really not all that hot, Nancy. Most of our people do better that that." Nancy's self-esteem was just zapped. Her scale of "secretarial skills" was depreciated.

Sometimes the scale can be enhanced: we can move up. I once asked a group of people how they would rate themselves as cooks. I explained that a "10" is a gourmet cook and a "one" is a person who fails miserably to prepare edible food. One woman admitted that she was "probably about a three." When she explained some of her more spectacular failures in the kitchen (the time she blew up an egg in the microwave, for example), I asked another question: "How well do you cook Mexican food?" "Oh," she responded quickly, "on Mexican food, I'm probably a six." How quickly she moved up the scale when we defined the criteria more closely!

Low self-esteem follows from a simplistic either-or picture of the world. Like a child growing to adulthood, we benefit from getting a clearer picture of the world as it really is—a world of contrasts, relative conditions, and subtle shades of differences. The same holds true for our view of ourselves. Avoid simplistic labels; they are inaccurate and dangerous to your well-being.

> **TRY THIS:**   Make it a habit to reduce your either-or language. Use terms that help you appreciate the relative differences rather than absolutes. Rid your vocabulary of "-est" words (biggest, best, richest, fastest, etc.) except when absolutely necessary. Likewise, be careful of polar opposites like "winner-loser," "hero-bum," "success-failure," etc.).

The Case of the Invisible Accomplishments

So much of what people do, both in the home and on the job, seems routine and unsatisfying; it's just plain grunt work. Clothing carefully laundered today will soon be soiled again. Routine reports meticulously prepared seem to drop into some black hole in the office. Paperwork and workplace clutter sprout like weeds in an untended garden.

It's up to us to decide what gives us self-esteem. No one can tell us what should be satisfying. We decide. Some people take enormous satisfaction from completing mundane tasks. Others make games of routine work, competing against their past performance. Still others relish everyday chores as a break from the usual work. For example, some days I actually *enjoy* doing the dishes. It's a task that can be relaxing, and unlike teaching or consulting where the results come later, I can see an immediate pay-off.

> **TRY THIS:**   Jot down some ideas on how you can make some of your mundane tasks into games you'd enjoy playing.

I have identified several barriers to strong self-esteem, among them the 80/20 reversal, the misdirected negative, the jealous negative, the inaccurate negative, and the silent treatment. I discussed some special challenges often faced by women, the relationship between language use and self-esteem, and the invisible accomplishment.

If you have been the victim of these negatives, it is easy to understand why you probably don't feel as good about yourself as you deserve to feel. However, to be aware of the cause is the first step towards corrective action.

People who are the most confident and satisfied are those who have developed unshakable self-love. Their basket is full to the brim. This unconditional love is deepened with the discovery of excelling at something and by then developing this area. As a result, they feel good about their own accomplishments, they receive praise and reward for their efforts, and they experience a satisfying level of self-esteem. It is this confidence that permits them to bounce back from any setbacks.

For some people, confidence was a gift of childhood bequeathed by nuturing parents who helped build a firm foundation of self-love and self-trust. For these fortunate individuals, the job is to strengthen self-esteem. They need to keep that love basket full.

Others, and this probably includes most of us, did *not* feel self-confident as children. Quite the contrary: we experienced a devastating lack of self-confidence then, which we have carried into adulthood. This psychological baggage causes us to remember negative comments heard long ago, and we act as though these comments are still valid. For example, if we spill something, we may chalk it up to an innate "clumsiness," simply because as children we had been labeled as clumsy so regularly.

TRY THIS: List some of the charges made against you as a child about which you are still sensitive. Especially be aware of those your parents or other opinion leaders told you. Are their charges valid today or do they needlessly hold you back?

Nine Steps to Winning the Confidence Game

The good news is that we, as adults, can take control and become powerfully self-confident by playing the Confidence Game.

The Confidence Game features nine simple but powerful ideas that will help you build the positive self-esteem necessary to bounce back from life's setbacks. You are in control. You are in charge of creating your own self-esteem. Now is the time to begin.

STEP 1: Talk to Yourself (It's really quite sane)

From this moment on, your opinion of yourself is the most important opinion. So make it a positive one. Since those around you will never tell you how wonderful you are nearly often enough, learn to tell yourself. Give yourself a pat on the back for a job well done. Compliment yourself on your appearance. Applaud your achievements. You are only giving yourself what you deserve, so say it out loud.

We all talk to ourselves constantly. Unfortunately, experts estimate that as much as 77 percent of everything we say to ourselves each day is negative and works against us. Yet, with a little discipline, we can turn the tables on negativity and use the power of verbal programming to our advantage. It's really quite simple. Just listen to what you are saying to yourself. Then give it a positive, upbeat, and optimistic twist.

When you hear yourself say, "You just screwed up again," rephrase that remark in a positive way. You can say, "Okay, I'm going to learn from that episode and do it differently next time." When you succeed at something—anything—give youself a verbal pat on the back for a job well done.

View your mind as a computer. Look to see what's stored there. If the information that your mind stores about you is negative, delete it.

In addition to complimenting yourself on specific matters, make it a point to say simply "I like myself" at least 25 times a day. It may sound a little weird, but trust me—it's okay. In fact, it's very healthy. Let's try it right now.

> I like myself
> I like myself
> I like myself . . .

Has a nice ring doesn't it? Say it often. Say it with *feeling. Mean it.*

TRY THIS: Set a goal to tell yourself explicitly that you like yourself: I will make it a point to say "I like myself" at least _____ times daily. I will do this (when?):

STEP 2: Expect Respect (You deserve it)

Those around you will treat you with as much respect as you demand. We attract to ourselves the kinds of people and circumstances that we feel we deserve. Each of us deserves respect, so don't allow yourself to be treated with anything less.

Develop some assertiveness skills. Speak up when you have an opinion. Make yourself heard diplomatically but firmly when you deserve a promotion. Speak up when you feel unfairly treated—or even when someone attempts to cut in front of you in line. Others won't dare treat you with less respect than you have for yourself.

Remember, assertiveness is not aggressiveness. We are assertive when we simply voice our thoughts and feelings honestly. Name calling isn't necessary and, in fact, produces more heat than light. For example, if someone offends you, don't say, "Pete, you're a dork" (even though that may be true). Instead, say, "Pete, what you are saying makes me angry." That's assertiveness. Share your honest feelings with another and they will be accepted as genuine.

TRY THIS: Identify one person who fails to give you the respect you deserve. What could you say to him or her?

STEP 3: Teach Others to Treat You Well

Explain the 80/20 reversal problem to people close to you, friends and family members. Tell them that it would be helpful to you if they would tell you when they notice things about you that they like as well as when they notice things that irritate or concern them. Most people will be surprised to learn that they are not giving you the positive support you need and deserve.

For example, a discussion with your boss might sound like this: "Dave, I realize that it's part of your job to correct me when I'm doing something wrong, but could I ask a small favor? Would you also let me know when I'm on the right track? That would help me do a better job and make me feel good, too." Few people would refuse such a reasonable request.

STEP 4: Tell Others What You Like about Them (Create a winning cycle)

Think about the 80/20 reversal in your associations with others. Check to see if you are much quicker to offer a "constructive criticism" than an unconditional compliment. If so, try to balance your comments. Walk up to someone you've known for a long time and offer a nice compliment. Make it sincere and specific. Then walk away. They may be confused at first, but they'll like it, and you'll feel good, too.

To get into the habit of doing this, itemize specific compliments in your "to-do" list for tomorrow and everyday this week. Make it a daily goal to compliment someone. You'll make that person's day, and create a winning cycle that will surely come back to you.

When you begin to comment on the positive traits and actions of others, you begin to build their self-esteem. The better they feel about themselves, the more likely they are to bolster your self-confidence.

> **TRY THIS:** Set a goal to pay three to five sincere, unsolicited compliments each day for a week. Observe what happens to the people you compliment, yourself, and your relationships.

STEP 5: Learn to Excel at Something

While we need to accept ourselves unconditionally as worthy, we validate our self-worth through our accomplishments as well. It makes sense to "improve" your image of yourself by recognizing your strengths and talents.

TRY THIS: Take a personal inventory of your current and potential skills and talents. Spend some uninterrupted time listing all the things at which you excel or could excel. Force yourself to make the list as long as possible. Fill up several sheets—a whole tablet if possible—with your talents and potentials.

This list can help identify the most fruitful areas for boosting your self-confidence.

Next, identify three to five things from your list at which you really want to be good at. Be sure that these are things to which you're willing to devote considerable time and effort. Write your top three here:

#1 _____

#2 _____

#3 _____

Learn to focus your time on your areas of talent, the activities that give you the most satisfaction. As you improve at these activities, you give yourself the best internal strokes and attract the admiration of others. People like to be around winners.

The more time you can spend using your talents, the faster your confidence will grow. The payoff is almost immediate. Nothing increases self-esteem as quickly as developing your talents and skills.

STEP 6: Don't Strain Your Neck by Looking Back

Don't look back. We've all made mistakes; we've all done stupid things; we've all put our foot in our mouth at some time. But what's done is done. You can't fix the past, so agonizing over it won't do any good.

Likewise, don't be too eager to apologize. Too often people apologize for things over which they had absolutely no control. Some people even seem to seek opportunities for making apologies. It is, of course, appropriate to apologize when you hurt or offend someone (as we all do), but never apologize for *who you are*.

> **TRY THIS:**   Close your eyes and create a vivid image in your mind of a past mistake or embarrassing moment. Recall how it felt, even if it was painful. Then, make the picture in your mind fade and go black. Let the image die once and for all and never bring it back again.

STEP 7: Overcome the Fear of Failure

"Don't worry, be happy," goes the popular tune. Overcome fear. Things are *supposed* to go well. You are *supposed* to be happy. Sometimes, this is easier said than done.

The root cause of fear is uncertainty and anticipation of some dreaded outcome. Lee Iacocca recalls his father asking, "Lido, what were you really worried about a month ago? Six months ago? A year ago?" When Lee couldn't remember, the old man had made his point. The things we worry about most *JUST DON'T HAPPEN.* All that good worrying goes to waste! Tackle problems when you come to them. Don't worry in advance or agonize over the past. Live in the present.

Another approach to getting rid of fear is to confide in a trustworthy person about your fears and let him or her convince you how groundless they are. I regularly do this with my wife. I express some fear of failing, and she quickly informs me that my fear just doesn't make any sense. Typically, she cites my past successes as proof that the thing I fear most will never happen. This approach is extremely effective, but make sure that your confidant will keep confidences and offer you the support you need.

> **TRY THIS:**   Jot down two or three things that really worried you a year ago, six months ago, five years ago. What happened? If you are having a hard time recalling examples, don't worry. Most of what we worry about never comes to pass!

STEP 8: Enlarge Your Comfort Zone

While the fear of failure is common, the fear of *success* hounds many people, too. If your self-concept doesn't allow you to see yourself as a success and you do succeed, you'll be outside your psychological "comfort zone." The solution—make your comfort zone bigger.

Most of us have a mental image of how much money we are worth, for example. Some people see themselves as $30,000 a year folks, others as $300,000 a year. People who have made big money once can almost always do so again. Even if they lose their original earnings, they see themselves as being worth the kind of money they made in the past. Don't try to tell a sales rep who made $150,000 last year that he can't meet or beat that figure this year!

Even if you haven't made big money in the past, you can program your mind to see yourself as, for example, a $200,000 a year guy or gal. Tell yourself (and create mental images discussed in Chapter 5) to expand your comfort zone and create new possibilities.

> **TRY THIS:** Identify some of the limits of your comfort zone now. How much money can you make? What kinds of things can you have? What kinds of relationships can you enjoy? What levels of leadership can you assume?

STEP 9: Binge and Purge (This one may not be perfectly sane)

I debated whether or not to include this discussion, but I'm convinced that for some people it has value. In fact, new studies on the power of mental control suggest that mental binging and purging can be very effective for certain personality types.[1] By confronting our worst thoughts, they become more familiar and less powerful. I've done this, and it's worked for me.

When you feel really low, try an emotional binge and purge. Go where you can be alone and then yell, scream, bitch, and complain. Tell yourself what's wrong. Go ahead, say it out loud: "I'm a complete failure. I am so incredibly stupid. I don't have any friends. I'm a complete idiot. I always act like a donkey in front of people I try to impress," etc. Lie on the bed and pound your fists into the pillow.

[1] A summary of current thinking on obsessive behaviors appeared in Erica E. Goode, "Thoughts We Hate to Think," *U.S. News and World Report*, August 14, 1989, pp. 48-9.

Stomp up and down; kick your heels into the floor. Throw a genuine temper tantrum just like a three year old. Be sure to overstate everything—it won't be hard to do when you're in this kind of a mood. Blow everything out of proportion. Let all the venom spill out.

After acting in such an extreme fashion for a while, you'll probably start to feel ridiculous. You should. Rationality will regain a toehold in your consciousness. Your heels will hurt, and you may have a headache from screaming. Just pick yourself up, brush yourself off, and start afresh, having purged all the asinine thoughts from your mind. Say, "That feels better," and get on with your life.

For some people, crying works better. Go ahead and have a good cry. Flood the joint! Wallow in self-pity. What the heck, life isn't fair, and we have a right to cry about it now and then. Use the same exaggerated technique to generate as much suffering as possible.

The trick to purging, of course, is to use it sparingly *and then to regroup.* I know of many people who find this technique helpful. They report feeling refreshed and reinvigorated. It is, however, an extreme measure and should be used only as directed and not while driving or operating heavy equipment.

STEP 10: Reframing Thoughts (The silver-lining principle)

We really do control how we look at events. Some people naturally see the bright side of almost everything; others tend to see the dark side. Reframing is the process of consciously changing one perception for a more useful one.

Suppose that someone tells you that he had to pay $4000 in additional income taxes this past year. What could you say? "Wow, that's a bummer. Uncle Sam sure ripped you off." That's one option. But a response reframed in a positive way would be to say, "Lucky you, you must have had a good income last year! That's great!"

Below is a list of possible situations with both positive and negative framing:

- *An active, noisy child*

Negative framing: That kid's annoying; maybe he's hyperactive; I wish his parents would do something about him.

Positive framing: What an active, healthy kid! He seems to be having a good time, even though he's a little loud. It's good to see a child having fun.

- *Being terminated from a job*

Negative framing: I'm worried sick. Where will the money come from; I'm too old to start over; this is a disaster.

Positive framing: This is a challenge but one that could work out nicely. I don't have to worry about that long commute any more. I've always wanted to try my hand at _____. Now I have the opportunity to move to Arizona. Maybe now's the time to start my own business.

- *Experiencing a mild heart attack*

Negative framing: That scared the hell out of me. I know it's just a matter of time before I'll be struck down again. Life is the pits. I hate getting old.

Positive framing: That was a warning. I guess I've been running in the fast lane too long. Now I know what I need to be doing about my diet and exercise. I'll develop much better health habits now and enjoy a long, full life.

We choose how we wish to frame our experiences. Framing positively costs no more than framing negatively—and it feels a lot better.

TRY THIS: Reframe several recent negative experiences as positives.

Constantly work to change your mental image of yourself. Create a mental picture of your best self and then act accordingly. Strut your stuff, even if only to yourself. Hold your head high, your shoulders back, and stride confidently to meet the world. Treat yourself with respect: act as confidently as you deserve to be. Before you know it, that confidence will be more than a pose—it will be real!

A parting thought on self-esteem:

When cloth is woven from thread, the number of threads per square inch determines the quality and strength of the finished fabric. In building self-esteem, our goal is to strengthen our "fabric" by creating and cultivating self-love. Interweave your many successful experiences to create a sense of confidence. You can play and win the confidence game!

Specific Behaviors that Promote Self-Esteem
(☑ Check those you've tried)

☐ 1. **Talk positively to yourself.** Say "I like myself" (or a similar phrase in your own words) *out loud* at least 25 times each day. Speak also of your positive accomplishments. Praise your progress—with feeling!

☐ 2. **Jot down affirmations** (sentences or quotes) on note cards or in your planner, and review them several times a day. Some of the ideas in this chapter may work for you, but be on the lookout for other ideas worth repeating to yourself.

☐ 3. **Love yourself unconditionally and appreciate your personal uniqueness.** Again, gather pertinent quotes or write out your own thoughts for frequent review. Each of us is unique. No one has ever been quite like you or me, nor will they ever be. We are precious and irreplaceable.

☐ 4. **Discover your own true greatness** by giving some hard thought to the things you enjoy and do well. Also, list a few things you'd love to be able to do well—things on which you'd be willing to spend some time and effort. Then focus your efforts on the talents and activities that reward you most handsomely.

☐ 5. **Provide positive strokes to at least two other people** today and every day. Be specific in telling them what you like about them and why. Keep the comments totally positive—no sneaking in "left-handed compliments."

☐ 6. **Purge the old, useless files in the computer of your mind.** Each time a negative thought comes up, visualize the DELETE function and banish it forever. If you really become depressed, explain your fears to a trusted friend and ask him or her to help you see your situation more rationally. Remind yourself that most of what we worry about will never occur.

☐ 7. **Never look back.** The past is past—and beyond control. Today alone can be acted upon, so make the most of today and every day. If changes are needed, begin them now.

☐ 8. **Be firm with yourself.** Talk to yourself as might a kindly schoolmaster. Don't let your mind wallow in the rubbish of self-pity or self-criticism. Exert mental discipline, starting *now*.

☐ 9. **Practice positive reframing.** Look for the good side in all situations. Make this a habit.

☐ 10. **Review the 10 steps to a stronger self-esteem.** Decide which will bring you the best payoff and try them.

BEST IDEA 2

Do the Right Things

CHAPTER 2

TAP THE POWER OF YOUR DEEPEST BELIEFS _____

> *Some luck lies not in getting what you thought you wanted but in getting what you have, which once you have got it you may be smart enough to see it is what you would have wanted had you known.*
>
> —Garrison Keillor

> *Ignore what you really desire and you ignore your greatest source of power.*
>
> —Author

Right out of high school, Marv started working as a teller in a large bank. He performed the job well, and after a year he was promoted to a position in customer relations. Three years later, he was offered a job as a loan officer. Since it was the natural next step, he accepted the position and did well for several years but always felt a vague sense of dissatisfaction.

One evening at a party the discussion turned to why each person had chosen his or her profession. As he listened to other peoples' reasons, Marv realized that he had never really *chosen* his work but had merely accepted a job. His older sister Danielle worked at the same bank, and it had seemed like an "okay" place to work. His career happened by default. It had never occurred to Marv that he could and should decide for himself the kind of work he would most *enjoy and find most satisfying.* After all, work is what you do eight hours a day so you can enjoy the rest of the day!

Marv's personal life was similarly undirected. He dutifully fulfilled all the expectations set for him: he had married a woman who was a lot like mom, and they had started a family and joined the right civic groups. It was as though he were acting out a script written by someone else. Marv never considered what *he* really wanted to do. No wonder he always felt a certain emptiness in his life. Marv often thought, "If it wasn't for Tuesday night bowling, life would be the total pits."

Marv's problem is one of self-direction. He seems to have none. He's living life by default. He has forfeited his control to unseen forces. To be in control implies having a clear idea of where we are going. Eight out of 10 people haven't a clue. They have never articulated a deep-felt sense of what they want from life. They may have asked themselves, "What's it all about, Alfie?" but they didn't listen carefully for the answers! They haven't defined what they value. They have not identified what is important to their success and happiness.

Unarticulated values leave one feeling rootless. We drift without an anchor and often question our self-worth. If you'd guess that Marv lacks self-esteem, you'd be right.

When people are unaware of their personal values—and the vast majority of people are—they find themselves playing roles and acting out scripts they didn't write. They play to an unseen audience, assume poses, and adopt social roles, responding always in ways they think meet the expectations of others.

W. Wesley Tennyson has observed that such behavior can be psychologically damaging. "Too often, the individual's role performance may be less than honest. The role one assumes may not be in accord with deepest desires and beliefs, or one may feel the need always to suppress the real self. The performance becomes an end in itself. And to use oneself in this way builds a tenuous base upon which to build or maintain an identity. Such motivation hinders the development of relations which promote growth and change, leading in some circumstances to individuals losing contact with their actual selves."

Core values come from feelings, not from someone else's notion of what should or ought to be. For example, you may have been taught that it is wise to avoid debt, but until you sense how great it can feel to be debt-free, this is not likely to become one of your core values.

All of us carry snapshots in our mind. When we think about them, sometimes we can feel the way we did when the picture was taken. Can you recall some special memories? They needn't be monumental events. I have a vivid picture in my mind of that cozy feeling when fall comes and the days grow shorter and the weather cooler. I see a snapshot of my family eating dinner in the kitchen—a simple dinner of home-made soup and bread. It's gray and blustery outside, but there's a fire in the fireplace.

I also carry a mental snapshot of Christmas Eve in our home, that special Hawaii vacation, a particularly good feeling when I got my first A in a college course, and the thrill of seeing my first book come out in print. These are memories that anchor values.

TRY THIS: **What I Feel Good About**

Conjure up some especially pleasant experiences from the past. Imagine these as snapshots in your mind that come to life. Describe several scenes in detail. What do they feel like? Smell like? Taste like? Sound like?

Then relate each of these to one of your core values.

Why Clear Values Are Critical to Success

If we ignore what we truly desire—what we really feel good about—we ignore our greatest source of power. When we fill our lives with activities and attitudes that are congruent with our core values, we achieve much. When we are unclear about our values, we cannot tap this power source. Instead, we experience anxiety, frustration, and unhappiness.

In top corporations, managers take heed of organizational values. In the runaway best-seller about highly successful organizations, *In Search of Excellence,* authors Tom Peters and Robert Waterman report that their "one, all-purpose bit of advice" to help organizations achieve excellence is this:

> Figure out your value system. Decide what your company stands for... Put yourself out 20 years in the future: What would you look back on with the greatest satisfaction?

That advice is equally sound for individuals. The challenge to clarify values applies to leaders in civic groups, church groups, families, and those of us interested in bouncing back from career setbacks or slumps.

Clarifying your value system can be the most constructive mental activity you will *ever* engage in.

What Are Personal Core Values?

A value is any concept that is intrinsically desirable. A *personal* value is one that *you* value.

Phrased another way, our values are *those things to which we are willing to devote ourselves.* They are the very essence of our being, for they *define what we see as worthwhile.* Upon them, we base *our standard of ethics.*

Personal values need no outside validation. They are strictly up to the individual, although we cannot condone values that are antisocial or destructive to others. The person who values something that society simply cannot allow—say he gets a warm feeling about armed robbery—will meet stiff resistance and may spend a lifetime being very frustrated—or rotting in jail!

When talking about values in seminars, I ask a participant this question: "Imagine that I placed a 10-foot-long plank here on the floor and asked you to walk across it. If you do, I'll give you $10. Would you do it?"

"Of course," is the typical reply.

Next, I ask another hypothetical question: "Imagine now that the same plank is placed between the tops of two skyscrapers. Would you still walk across it for $10?"

Of course, they say, "No way!"

Now, imagine another scenario: The plank still extends between the skyscrapers, but instead of my waving the $10 bill on the other side, I now hold your child upside down by his ankles over the edge and say I'll drop him if you don't walk across the plank. (Sinister fellow, ain't I?)

What's your response now?

Some wise-cracking participants may ask "Which child?" but most say that they would readily risk their own lives to save their offspring. This reflects a core value. Many of us would readily risk our lives for—or *give* our lives for—our children. We have a bone-deep core value that says our children are worth *any* sacrifice we can make for their well-being. Even walking the plank!

Unhappy people, or those in a slump, typically have little or no clear awareness of their bone-deep beliefs. They may profess to believe in results that can be easily measured, such as earnings, promotions, and games won. But these aren't values. These are targets to hit. Value-directed people want to know *why* they should even aim at the target. They express their bone-deep beliefs in such terms as "personal growth," "self-esteem," and "satisfaction."

Likewise, value-directed people *discuss* their values, often citing stories of how they, or others, acted in ways congruent with their beliefs. The British Olympic runner depicted in the movie *Chariots of Fire,* who refused to compete on Sunday—even when requested to do so by royalty—made a powerful statement about his religious values. He drew the line; his personal ethic was clear.

My friend Sharon provides another example. She was doing a great job as a manager of a retailing firm when she re-examined her personal values and discovered that she genuinely preferred to be a full-time mother, especially while her children were in elementary school. Her decision to leave her job posed some economic challenges for her family, but with some creativity and belt-tightening, they managed and Sharon felt better about herself and her life. Her choice is not the one all women would make; nevertheless, it was *her* choice and it was value-based. The decision she made moved her in the direction of being in harmony with her values.

How Most People Define Success

All people seek success, yet each has a unique definition of the term. In a national survey, people cited the following factors as their criteria for personal success, ranked from the most important to least important:

- Good health
- Enjoyable job
- Happy family
- Peace of mind
- Good friends
- Intelligence
- Unlimited money
- Talent
- Luck
- Luxury car
- Expensive home[1]

---

[1] Reported in Roger Fritz, *Nobody Gets Rich Working for Somebody Else* (New York: Dodd, Mead & Company, 1987), p. 243.

> **TRY THIS:** Rank the list of the definitions of success by your priorities, numbering your choices 1 through 11 from most to least important. To what extent does your ranking match with the list above? What might help account for differences?

Common to most people's definition of success are the following requirements:

1. **Peace of mind.** We succeed when we are comfortable with ourselves, because we are essentially free from fear, anger, and guilt. We generally like ourselves.
2. **Health and vigor.** We succeed when we can maintain a reasonable level of physical wellbeing. Although we have natural limitations and sometimes handicaps, we make the best of the physical capabilities we possess. We take care of our physical selves.
3. **Loving relationships.** We succeed when we love and are loved by others. Our relationships are free of debilitating hatred or resentment toward others.
4. **Financial freedom.** We succeed when we have sufficient money so that we do not worry about covering our needs. We also have sufficient funds to avoid the enslavement of excessive debt.
5. **Worthy goals.** We succeed when we have a sense of what is important, and we are making reasonable progress toward accomplishment.
6. **Feelings of personal fulfillment.** We succeed when we are what the psychologists call "self-actualized," doing things of worth that provide us with personal satisfaction.

Success quite literally happens when we feel good about our *progress toward* these six goals. Notice the critical phrase "progress toward."

Ben Franklin's Clarification Process (This is better than the kite trick)

The idea of value clarification isn't new. Benjamin Franklin described in his autobiography how he clarified his personal values. After many years of being unsuccessful, bouncing from job to job and city to city—

he lived in Boston and New York before he went to Philadelphia—at the age of 28, Franklin finally said to himself, or words to this effect: "I'm going to sit down and describe my core values, the values that are going to shape my life from now on."

He underwent a thoughtful process, one that took some time and considerable effort. Finally, he wrote and described 12 critical values around which he committed to shape his entire life. "No more lack of direction for his guy," said Ben (I'm paraphrasing again).

As he worked through the process of defining his values, he showed his notes to a friend, a Quaker. The man reviewed the list and said, "Ben, those are 12 good values. They are worthwhile attributes to develop in your life. Let me just suggest, though, that there might be one other value you'll want to add." He talked Benjamin Franklin into adding a thirteenth value: humility.

Many years later, at the age of 81, Benjamin Franklin reported in his autobiography that he felt that he had finally achieved a sense of *oneness* with his values. Of all his illustrious accomplishments, Franklin felt especially good about achieving oneness, balance, and a sense of peace that resulted from feeling in harmony with the values he had articulated for himself years before.

He didn't arrive at that point in a few months—or even a few years. But he did get there eventually because of his persistent focus on his well-clarified values.

As an interesting footnote, Franklin reported that he had become congruent with 12 of the 13 values. I bet you can guess which one didn't make the list (right, the one that wasn't his to begin with—humility).

Clear Values Are Crucial to Personal Excellence

Setbacks and slumps in people's careers or personal lives can often be traced to a lack of clear values. Without a conscious awareness of our heartfelt beliefs, we are much more likely to gallop off in different directions according to whim. Without knowing our values, managing our lives becomes little more than choosing among equally worthy, or unworthy, activities. Without knowing our values, we become subject to the tyranny of the immediate; we react to outside pressures rather than doing what's most meaningful to us.

And we seldom do as good a job as we could. We function as workers instead of craftsmen, hired help instead of proprietors.

Values clearly articulated should serve as the compass for our journey. They point the way, giving meaning, purpose, and opportunity for satisfaction.

Sorting Out Values Isn't Easy

If value clarification were easy, more people would do it. But it isn't and they don't. One reason for the difficulty of the task is that values can conflict with each other, even though both are desirable.

For example, an employee's need to maintain friendships by socializing with his co-workers (that's good) and the need to tend to his work (another good thing) are potentially in conflict. Likewise, the need to allow our children the freedom to make choices (that's good) even though we'd like to protect them from the high cost of their mistakes (that's good, too). Which is more important, socializing or finishing every task? The freedom to choose or avoiding mistakes? Earlier, we saw that Sharon placed more value in personally rearing her young children than in pursuing her career.

Putting Value Clarification to Work

Value clarification is a powerful way to help break out of a slump or bounce back from a setback. I challenge you to clarify your values, to seek out what is most important in your life, your core values, your personal ethics. Devote some thoughtful time to the process. It can do wonders for rejuvenating your will.

TRY THIS: **Building a Rough Draft**

The activities listed below will help you articulate *your* core values. Take some time to answer these questions thoughtfully and honestly.

1. What are your greatest professional and personal abilities or skills? At what do you excel?

2. What kinds of activities are you not good at and would prefer to avoid? Give examples from both your work and your personal life.

3. What are your major professional and personal goals for the next 12 months? (Name two or three in each category below.)

   Professional   Health/Physical

   Family or Relationships   Financial

   Mental/Spiritual   Other

4. Describe your life 20 years from now, in detail.

   Where will you live?
   What will you be doing?
   What assets will you own?
   What activities will you spend your day doing?

   (use a separate sheet)

The exercise above should force you to identify your priorities. There are, of course, no "right" or "wrong" answers, only what is true for you. To clarify your values further, read on:

TRY THIS: Determine Where You Stand

The next few pages offer activities to help you clarify your values further. First, take a few moments to read through the list of selected values. Consider each of these and the degree to which it seems important to you. You will probably give your values different names later. This list is not intended to be complete but is provided to stimulate thought.

As you read through the list, assign these values into three categories: values you *endorse* (+), those you *reject* (−), and those that are *neutral* (0)—you are neither for nor against them.

Many of the values listed may sound good to you. Force yourself to make some choices. *Do not endorse a value unless you would be willing to dedicate a significant amount of your time and energy to it.*

I value . . .

career success	wealth
total honesty	honoring commitments
religious activity	knowing the right people
social correctness	productivity
open mindedness	serving those less fortunate
individualism	fame in my profession
winning	caring for others
family success	being well groomed
being law abiding	health and vigor
loyalty	keeping good records
order	being a leader
balance	mentoring others
having many friends	intellectual growth
having many skills	trust in God
discipline	tolerance of others
persuasiveness	being witty, clever
social activity	financial security
emergency preparedness	being artistic
athletic excellence	being a good team player
pride in my city	self-sufficiency
musical excellence	dressing for success
awareness of my heritage	accuracy
projecting a good image	being influential
honoring parents	government involvement
building things	caring for animals
thrift	

Here's the next step in the clarification process: Look back over your endorsed and rejected values and rank the top four you endorse most vigorously and the top four you reject most vigorously.

My top four endorsed values:

1.

2.

3.

4.

My top four rejected values:

1.

2.

3.

4.

Now some other tough questions: Do you honestly spend a major portion of your productive time working to achieve your top four values? Do you spend time and effort moving toward congruence with values you *reject?* Do you seem to get tangled up in activities related to values that are neutral to you?

Often, people can quickly identify situations in which they are spending a lot of time chasing after things they reject and fail to chase those of real value to them.

Take one more look at your lists. Circle any values that seem to conflict with your actions—either things you value but don't do much about or things you do but don't really value.

Values Can Change

Keep in mind that values can change. Often we value something more strongly in one phase of our life than in another. An example of this comes from Steve Wozniak, co-founder of Apple Computer, Inc.

A recent story tells how Steve now spends much more of his time bicycling across Yellowstone Park and reading books. He says he has "reclaimed a life from the high-pressure world of high tech."

"I want to change my life to where I have a normal life after 10 years of being chased by everyone in the world. . .I've been a very patient person with all the things that have gone on for many years. I've been very accessible. I've been giving. But in the last year and a half it really started to bother me. I'm ready to be me."

Since fulfilling his childhood dream of designing a computer, Wozniak is now ready to try his hand at teaching. He doesn't have a full-time teaching job, but he has enlisted as a volunteer at a tiny school in the Santa Cruz Mountains. He wants to teach children to follow their creative urges and be more nonconformist and unconventional.

Wozniak left Apple with $100 million in stock, which makes it quite a bit easier for him to be a free spirit. Nevertheless, he seems to be turning his life toward a new level of congruence with his core values. His story also illustrates how values can change.

Remember, pressing needs can distort your true values. If you are broke, you may place a disproportionate emphasis on making money; but once you can again meet your needs comfortably, making money may become less urgent. Likewise, if your personal relationships are in a mess or your health and vigor slipping, you may find it tough to focus on less pressing but ultimately as important values.

TRY THIS: **Name that Value**

Now that you have identified some tentative core values, let's sharpen your idea of what they mean. Three steps will help you name and clarify your values:

1. Name your value.
2. Describe what it means.
3. Identify activities aligned with this value (covered in Chapter 3).

As you sharpen your focus, select a label or name for each value. Make sure that the name is one you're comfortable with.

For example, Paul worked through the value clarifying process and identified these seven values: *health and vigor, financial security, family unity, leadership, personal success, spiritual growth,* and *life-balance.* Paul feels comfortable with these labels. Your labels will probably be different. Select whatever names you wish for your values. (You can name a value "Fido," if that's meaningful to you.) Go ahead, write three values on the worksheet below.

plan·it
life organizer

Life Plan

Core Values	Value Aligning Activities

The second step is to *describe* in writing, using the present tense, how you feel when you are congruent with a particular value. Specifically what will you be doing and thinking when your life reflects this value? For example, in describing his life congruent with *health and vigor,* Paul wrote the following statements:

I exercise regularly and avoid harmful habits.
I maintain reasonable weight.
I get regular physical and dental check-ups.
I maintain vigor by daily planning, goal setting, and rewarding myself for accomplishments.
I jog, play racquetball, swim, play golf, and occasionally do wild and crazy things to let off steam.
I refuse to let stress grind me down.
I avoid excessive worry.
I view life as fun and full of opportunities.

Notice that the statements are all in the present tense. This is important. Even though Paul may not yet be doing all that he says he'll do to be value-congruent, he describes his actions as if he were already there.

Here's another value described:

Under the value of "financial security," Chris writes the following statements:

I can afford all that we need, as well as a few luxuries.
I vacation with my family and my wife each year.
I have no debts. Even my home is paid for. And my income is secure.
I have a plan for my retirement and adequate insurance.
I have good, income-producing investments.
We are secure but not extravagant.

Again, keep in mind that these are statements of where Chris *expects* to be when he's achieved congruence with the value he labeled "financial security."

To reap the greatest benefits from these activities, I recommend that initially you spend several hours writing, clarifying, and describing your values. Once recorded, you will no doubt sharpen and refine these as you go through the phases of your life. *You are not locked into these values forever!* Things change. But meanwhile, your values provide the rudder for steering your personal ship toward the ports you have selected.

Place the finished version of your values sheets in a notebook for frequent reference. I recommend the "Plan-It Life Organizer,"[3] which I developed as a tool for tying together values, goals, and daily activities in one convenient format for frequent reference.

What this Process Will Do for You

Just as well-managed and successful organizations are value-based, so are super-achieving people. Clarified values provide a foundation that takes much of the guesswork out of their decisions. They know where to spend their valuable time, energies, and talents. They can better identify exactly where to bounce back from life's inevitable temporary setbacks.

Clarifying your values can place you ahead of at least 80 percent of the people in the world. You can truly achieve the racer's edge—that extra degree of success that jumps you from the middle of the pack to the top 10 or top one percent in any field you choose—simply by knowing at a gut level exactly what you value in life.

In any organization, we typically find that 20 percent of its members account for 80 percent of its success. In sales, for example, this means that the top 20 percent of sales reps make more sales than the remaining 80 percent. Statistics show that their rewards are commensurate with their results; for example, the top 20 percent of sales people can expect earnings 16 times greater than the bottom 80 percenters.

---

[3] I developed the Plan-It Life Organizer several years ago to provide a convenient system for recording values, goals, and daily activities in such a way as to give users the power of focus. Other planner systems can be adapted in some cases, but if you'd like to try the Plan-It, ordering information appears in the back of this book.

Carried one step further, the top 20 percent of the top 20 percent groups (in other words, the top four percent of the company) can expect to earn 54 times as much as the average bottom 80 percenter!

The point is that those who distinguish themselves receive significantly greater rewards than those who muddle along with the "average" majority. Breaking out of the pack is almost always a matter of doing *just a little bit more,* sticking with it *just a little bit longer*—in other words, providing the racer's edge. Value-based activities are those worth sticking with and putting your whole self into. You'll do so cheerfully because of their importance to you.

Value clarification and its first cousin, goal setting, make a tremendous difference in personal and professional success. This is a documented fact. Every top achiever knows this.

By applying your precious, limited time and effort to those things that make a difference, you learn to work smart, not just hard. You get the very most possible from your efforts. And, given a realistic perception of control, clear set of values, and persistent effort to become one with those values, you cannot fail.

Specific Behaviors that Build the Value Focus Habit
(☑ Check off when you've tried them)

☐ 1. Take some time to work and rework the activities suggested, giving careful, thoughtful consideration to each. Find a quiet place, get off by yourself, and tune out the rest of the world for a day if you can. Then use discipline to focus your energies on the critical question of your core values.

☐ 2. Get away with your spouse (or partner) and talk about your shared values. Work through the steps of naming and articulating what each means. Build a consensus on what's important for your family. Then, if appropriate, take a value list to your children and see if they feel good about them. What you can end up with is a "family charter" that can provide a base for important family decisions. Ask the kids if they can agree with these family decisions. Get them to sign the charter and use it as a basis for family discussions periodically.

☐ 3. Try the family charter approach with workers or members of organizations you are involved in. Workers and employers gain a solid sense of common mission from this approach, as long as you don't hammer your own ideas down others' throats.

☐ 4. Refer to your "Life Plan" (values) sheets at least once a week. Especially review them when setting new goals for the month or year to check for congruence.

☐ 5. Write your values on 3″×5″ cards and carry them around with you. Memorize them. Share them with others who would be supportive. Talk about your values. Live them. In doing so, they truly become the personal power source that will generate your encore!

CHAPTER 3

REDISCOVER SELF-MASTERY ─────────────────

Our plans miscarry because they have no aim. When a man does not know what harbor he is making for, no wind is the right wind.

—Seneca

The vast majority live by default, not knowing where they want to go, having no need to figure out how to get there. Not specifying their goals, they have no plans to follow, no new habits to develop, no behaviors to rehearse, and no strategies to revise and update. . .The mind trips out into tension-relieving, rather than goal-achieving activities.

—Denis Waitley[1]

You have achieved much. Even if you are now experiencing a setback or slump, there is no denying past successes. You've had a bunch of them. And the achievements of the past are prologue to the good things to come.

Goals really are the bedrock of any success program. But too often, the process losses something in the application. People oversimplify setting goals. They confuse goal setting with wishing or daydreaming.

I've worked toward goals for many years, and I am still constantly revising my approach. What seems to be a simple activity is really very complex. There are many things to understand about goals. Sometimes we need to peel off the top layers of our understanding to reach where they really start to work for us.

─────────────
[1]Denis Waitley, *The Double Win* (Old Tappan, NJ: Fleming H. Revel Company, 1985), p. 119.

How Mastery Is Achieved

Have you ever helped a toddler learn to catch a ball? How did you do it? Most folks do it by first handing the baby the ball. (Look at that cute toothless grin.) Now we'll try tossing it lightly from a few inches away. "Good baby—you caught it!" Now we'll back up a little farther until the distance increases and the speed of the throw picks up. Eventually, the child feels comfortable catching a ball.

Every major league shortstop started out that way. No ball player took a major league fastball as his very first catch. And none of us, facing a new task or challenge, should be expected to match the skills needed without some short-term little successes to teach us.

Every skill is learned one small step at a time. We learn to succeed one small success at a time. The old cliché could not be more accurate: Success literally breeds success. Little wins lead to more and bigger victories. If you haven't had any little wins lately, it's time for you to start making some happen.

In training seminars, I discuss goals and their achievement. I do this because having goals is absolutely critical to mastering the kinds of skills which, in turn, are absolutely critical to bouncing back. New situations usually call for some new goals.

Much has been written about goal setting. We have all heard the familiar litany: set realistic short- and long-term goals, direct your energies toward their accomplishment, and you will succeed. Great motivational speakers, like Zig Ziglar and others, focus almost their entire career on teaching goals.

Why are successful people so intent on goals? Why does goal setting work? It works because goals give direction to life. They show us what harbor we are making for. They provide points of reference. And to reach them involves self-mastery.

Goals as Points of Reference

A farmer was plowing his field out in the wide open plains of southern Idaho. As he began his first furrow, he looked for some distant point as a marker. At first, he could find no landmark on the horizon—no tree, no building—but he finally saw an indistinguishable black object on the horizon and decided to use it as a reference point. After plowing for some distance, he happened to look back; to his dismay, he saw that his furrow was wavy. He climbed off the tractor and approached the black object. When he got close enough, he realized why he had a problem. The object was a large jackrabbit!

If our goal is a moving target instead of something fixed or permanent, we should expect unpredictable results. So let's fix a point of reference that's dependable—let's cage the rabbit!

When a goal is fixed and permanent, it can serve as a measure of our success. Reaching it, in turn, becomes the motivator that pushes us toward further goals.

Characteristics of Good Goals

A goal is a powerful force when it meets six criteria. Effective goals should be:

- **Concrete and specific**—phrased clearly.
- **Vivid** and **exciting to our senses.**
- **Realistic**—they should stretch us, but not beyond the bounds of what is reasonable.
- **Measurable** in some quantitative and/or qualitative way; **target dates** for achievement should be set.
- **Written**—an unrecorded goal is only a wish.
- **Value-anchored**—our goals should be congruent with our values.

Let's Make this Perfectly Clear

Concrete and specific goals are ones that conjure up clear pictures in your mind. To do so, their language must be clear. The goals should be phrased as *positive* statements:

Poor phrasing:	Lose weight and avoid fattening food. Don't make any billing errors (negative wordings).
Better phrasing:	Have a lean body of 121 pounds by September 1.

or

Eat fresh fruits and vegetables twice each day instead of fried foods.

or

Produce 100% correct bills for April.

Avoid negative wording because the mind rebels against negation. For example, if I tell you: "Do not think of an elephant," what's the first thing that pops into your mind? Of course, that elephant! Increasing clarity won't help as long as the thought is phrased negatively: "Don't think of a large, yellow elephant with pink polka dots dancing on his hind legs" conjures up precisely that ludicrous vision, in part *because* it is so vivid!

Moreover, a negative statement does not convey as much information as a positive one. If I say, "She does NOT live on Main Street," what information do you have? You can eliminate one possible place where you thought she might live, but you're still in the dark as to where she *does* live. Conveying much more is the positive, "She lives on Maple Street."

So, for clarity, use *positive* statements. And the more *specific* the statement, the better. "She lives at 321 Maple Street, Apartment 4-B" would work nicely.

For goals to be achieved, they should be clearly and positively worded. They should also *excite the senses*.

Excite the Senses

A powerfully conceived goal is one that you can mentally see, hear, touch, taste, feel, and even smell. The more your senses can be stimulated by the goal, the more powerful the goal.

For example, suppose your goal is to become president of your company. What will that feel like? To make your goal powerful, you need to imagine vividly exactly how it will be. What will you feel like when you come to work in your new role? What will the office be like? What will be its colors (the rug, walls, paintings), textures (the feel of your new executive chair), smells (the coffee your secretary brings you, the scent of the leather-covered furniture), sounds (your phone ringing and your secretary speaking your name), sights (from your office window)?

The more you can stimulate senses, the more powerful the goal. Also, use your senses to anticipate the rewards you'll receive for achieving your goal. And as you progress toward the major goal, reward yourself regularly for achieving those small victories en route.

The Power of Linking Realistic Expectations and Goals

Many people perceive as a dilemma having ambitious goals reflecting their true potential, yet wanting to be realistic about possibilities. For example, for a 70-year-old man with no political experience or advanced education to announce suddenly that he wants to become a U.S. senator would seem unrealistic, naive, or just plain silly. The same goal for a younger man or woman—a university student for example— would also be ambitious and yet not unrealistic as a long-term target.

The problem, of course is what economists call "scarce resources." There are only 100 U.S. senators, of whom approximately one-third are elected or reelected every two years. The limit upon the number of opportunities to become a senator is thus severely restricted. Senators will always remain a very elite group.

Having unrealistic expectations leads to frustration. When we expect too much from ourselves, or from others, we are setting ourselves up for failure.

Be realistic. I know this advice may seem to contradict the advice in some of the "positive-thinking" books you may have read. But I'd much rather see people set *realistic* targets, based on *realistic* expectations, and have the satisfaction of accomplishing the "do-able" rather than banging their heads against an unforgiving wall of the "un-do-able." The slump you are now experiencing may, in fact, be the result of having had unrealistic goals.

If our same 70-year-old would-be senator announced that he will become president of his own small company, we, and more importantly, *he* would be much more likely to believe in his goal. There are far more positions for new company presidents.

How can you tell if an expectation is realistic? Answering these questions can help you assess whether it is realistic or not:

- Is what I expect within the realm of human ability, as I have experienced it in the past?
- Is the desired outcome subject to the problem of scarcity? Is there enough of the desired goal to go around or few enough people competing for it?

And perhaps the most important question,

- Am I willing to pay the price for the desired outcome?

Realistic expectations are powerful propellants to success, while irrational expectations bear the seeds of folly and disappointment. As H. L. Mencken put it, "The most costly of all follies is to believe passionately in the palpably not true."

Contrary to the simplistic views of some people who profess to believe in "positive thinking," we cannot achieve everything we want simply by writing down a goal and "thinking hard" about it. We are all to some degree limited by natural forces. We may, for example, come up short in body coordination, thus ruling out a career as a professional athlete. Likewise, we all differ in our mental capacity and ways of thinking. Sometimes natural limitations block us from being something we'd like to be, and all the positive thinking in the world isn't going to change that.

Please don't construe my thoughts to mean that you should set your goals low. Not at all. I suggest only that you temper them with a dose of reality—not pessimism or small thinking—just reality. Besides, once you've achieved today's realistic goal, you can set a new, higher goal for next year! If you want to be president, first get elected to a lesser office.

What we expect out of life has a powerful impact on what we get from it. If our early ambitions have been frustrated because we set too high a goal, our self-confidence may have been damaged. Conversely, if our early goal-setting was successful, then we can probably proceed with confidence.

Management of expectations includes ridding ourselves of the cruel delusion that we can do whatever we want to do and become whatever we want to be, even though we may lack the necessary mental capacity, training, talent, or physical ability. Don't sell your goals short, but keep them realistic.

You must decide if your limitations are imagined or real. But be prepared for the possibility that some are real. A sign seen at the Pentagon makes this point. It reads,

---

THEY TOLD HIM THAT IT COULDN'T BE DONE. HE ROLLED UP HIS SLEEVES AND WENT TO IT. HE TACKLED THE JOB THAT COULDN'T BE DONE— AND HE COULDN'T DO IT.

Okay, you're convinced that your goal is "do-able." Now what? Now, take its measure; see how it stacks up.

Make Your Goals Measure Up

Measurable goals are more clearly defined and, hence, achievable, than the nonmeasurable. To say you'd like to weigh 160 pounds is more specific than simply to say "I'd like to lose some weight." To say you will earn $85,000 this year is more specific than to say you'd like to make "some big bucks."

But be careful. All things cannot be easily described by a number, and just because they can't be doesn't mean that they should not be goals. I've known people who set goals to be "more at ease when speaking before groups" or to "feel closer to my spouse." These can be good goal areas even though they aren't quantifiable. Typically, however, these qualitative goals are attended by some specific behaviors—actions that can be counted or rated. Feeling closer to a spouse, for example, may manifest itself in having a special "date night" several times a month.

TRY THIS: What behaviors might indicate progress toward
accomplishing goals in the following areas?

Desired outcome   *How measured?*

Become physically fit
Be better informed
Better participation in meetings
Stronger relationship with kids
Feelings of personal growth
Less anxiety
(others—add your own)

One other thought about measuring. Try to avoid phrases like *"every
day* I will..." The problem with such wording is that if you miss just
one day, you may feel a failure and give up your goal.

Poor phrasing: Every day I will read one chapter in a self-help book.

or

Jog three miles each day.

Better phrasing: I will read 25 chapters in self-help books this month.

or

Jog 90 miles this month.

Deadlines as Energizers

A *deadline* is to a goal what a trigger is to a gun. People accomplish
more when a deadline looms; they suddenly feel a sense of urgency
that propels them toward accomplishment. Eighty percent of monthly
goals are accomplished in the last eight days of a month.

Make sure that your goals have the motivational triggers they need. Set realistic target dates both for the overall goal and, just as importantly, for the steps that need to be accomplished to reach it. For example, if the goal is to "build a $5 million distributorship," intermediate steps might be to sell $X worth of certain products by July 1; to recruit X number of effective subdistributors by August 1, etc.

Big Goals and Little Goals

It is easier to assign realistic target dates to specific, short-term tasks. If your long-range goal is to become a medical doctor, you'll want to set a rough date for getting your M.D. degree. For such a goal, the target date will be a particular year rather than a particular day.

Becoming a doctor is a major goal. It is long-range and requires many intermediate steps, each of which similarly requires subgoals. For example, this major goal requires completing pre-med college courses, successful scores on medical school applications, securing financing for school, etc.

The grander the goal, the more shorter-term tasks will be involved. As you analyze each task in detail, set targets for its accomplishment. By achieving these tasks, you work toward making your goal a reality.

Ultimately, for each of your goals, there should be some action you can take *today*. If financial security is important, do something toward it *today:* Open a bank account, make a payment toward a debt, or decide to toss all your lose change into a can—starting today. Regardless of how small the action, do *something*.

> **TRY THIS:**   Consider one of your long-term goals. Now write down one task you can do *today* to move you toward achieving that goal.

If It Isn't Written, It Isn't a Goal

People in my training sessions often say, "I have lots of goals, I just haven't written them down." My reaction: If a goal isn't written, it isn't a goal—it's a wish. Occasionally wishes come true, but not as often as goals can be achieved.

We reinforce our direction by reading our *written* goals. If not formulated in writing, the goal will change and eventually blow away like a summer cloud.

It is critical to write out both big and little goals. In addition, you should write these somewhere where you will look at them often. I recommend that they become a part of your daily calendar or planner system, where they will constantly remind you of your direction.

Goals Need Nurturing Roots: Values

Finally, a goal must be anchored in a *value.* In Chapter 2, I discussed values and now I'll tell you how to make your goals express your values. To do so, let's get romantic for a moment and talk about...

The Comfortable Marriage of Values and Goals

We achieve congruence with our core values by acting in accord with our values. Ultimately, we, like Ben Franklin, can achieve *total alignment*—the state where all that we do flows harmoniously from what we truly value. Since our values come from deep within, they provide exceptional motivation for achieving our goals.

To achieve total value alignment requires that we...

1. Know our core values
2. Focus our activities on these values
3. Direct our activities toward achieving big and little goals
4. Each day, act to advance toward our goal

Inner fulfillment, or *happiness,* comes from our ability to meet two needs:

1. The need to be **active** in doing things that have **meaning** to us
2. The need to feel a sense of **progress** or growth

Having values and goals steers us toward success and inner fulfillment. But the only real control we have is over our actions *now*. If what we are doing *now* has nothing to do with our core values and aligning activities, we are being ineffective. And, although we have all experienced times of being ineffective, the difference between success and failure is how well we can bounce back to personal effectiveness after having been in a slump.

TRY THIS: Setting Short-Term and Long-Term Goals

If you have not set goals before (or have stopped doing so), I suggest an activity I've used in training sessions:

On one side of a 3″×5″ card or slip of paper write out two or three simple tasks you've been meaning to do on your job or in your career preparation. Often, these are tasks you just don't seem to get around to doing.

(When people draw a blank, I suggest possibilities like "clean out middle desk drawer," "write for night school catalog," "read one chapter of a success book," or "start a budget book.")

Now, turn over the card and write on the other side two or three goals or tasks you could do in your personal, nonbusiness, life. (People somtimes use "take husband out to dinner," "play ball with Tommy for 15 minutes," "clean out the garage," "write a note to Mom," etc.)

Now here is your assignment: Carry this card with you, looking at it often. As you accomplish your goals, place a check mark next to them with a red felt-tip pen.

It's as simple as that to get a taste of success in achieving goals. People who have tried this soon find themselves writing out more goals and getting that good feeling of success from checking them off when they are realized.

Like the baby learning to catch the ball, we learn step by step and gain confidence from our history of accomplishing *written goals.* Soon we'll be playing shortstop in the majors.

Success Breeds Success

Obviously, there is more to setting goals than writing out random tasks on slips of paper. Many things we would like to accomplish are long-term goals requiring a major commitment of our time, effort, and other resources. Once accomplished, these grand goals go a long way to defining our personal greatness.

I know many people who could never be convinced that they *cannot* accomplish something. At the "gut level," they know that whatever they set their mind to becomes reality. And why should they doubt? They have a track record of *accomplishing* their goals. Because they have written out and then checked off achieving their goals, they can document their success.

I have been using a goal-setting system for about 20 years. I won't tell you that I made every goal I ever set. Nobody does that. But I can truthfully say that, using the process I've described to you, at least 80 percent of every target I set is achieved. Goal setting works!

Shaping Values

In Chapter 2, you began to clarify your values. Now, I will teach you a process for value *shaping*. Just as a sculptor shapes a block of stone by chipping and polishing, so we can shape our values by defining them in words, thoughts, and actions.

Let's work through an example. Take a blank sheet of paper or use the sample Life-Plan worksheet on page 79.[2]

First, select one of the core values you identified as important to you. Remember, you gave this value a name. The name you gave it should quickly elicit emotional and sensory responses that will help you focus on this value. Remember, this value is yours—you *own* it. It *works for* you.

---

[2] The Plan-It Life Organizer I developed includes "Life Plan" pages that provide spaces for the value-shaping activity described here. See the back of the book for information on ordering the Plan-It Life Organizer.

plan·it
life organizer

Life Plan	
Core Values	**Value Aligning Activities**

Next, write the name of this value in the left-hand column of the worksheet, as I did in the example below. After you have written the name of the value, use the present tense to describe what it will be like when you are *congruent* with that value. In other words, what will you be doing, thinking, and feeling when you've comfortably internalized that value?

The following is an example from my planner, using FAMILY UNITY as the selected value. (Note: I typed this only after several handwritten drafts.)

plan·it
life organizer

Life Plan

Core Values	Value Aligning Activities
FAMILY	
I cheerfully spend time with Helen & kids. I am sensitive to their needs; avoid depreciating comments; encourage them & help each of them develop a positive self-concept. I express affection often; I pray with and for them. I avoid losing my temper toward them. I teach them success principles.	* Family vacations each year * Help kids with goal-setting, self-management * Regular family home evening & activities * Stress our family values * Try to make home the best place to be & family members the best friends to have * Give kids success opportunities * Uplift, don't put down * Regular one-on-one time for talking with each child

Take your time. Visualize what your life will be like when you are really at peace with and totally in-tune with your chosen value. If you aren't there yet, that's normal. The important thing is to be *moving toward* value congruence. Writing in the present tense gives you a feel for what your life will be like when you are in congruence and this, in itself, enhances your motivation to make that value congruence a reality.

Here's another example, using the value heading, FINANCIAL SECURITY:

FINANCIAL SECURITY	
I can afford all that we need as well as a few luxuries. I vacation with the family & with Helen each year. I have no debts; even my home is paid for and my income is secure. I have planned for my retirement & have adequate insurance etc. I have good income-producing entities. We are secure but not extravagant.	* Be debt free by 1996; make extra principle paymts * Tax shelter 15%+ IRA * Careful investment; no speculation * Continue to build income-producing entities * Budget system & financial planning

Following is a summary of the three steps in basic value shaping:

1. Identify the value by name.
2. Use the present tense to describe what it feels like to be congruent with that value.
3. Describe value-aligning activities, phrased as goals.

A personal value system can be visualized as the foundation of a building. The goals and activities will be structurally sound only if the foundation is solid. Just as many of us have never really looked at the foundation of our house, most people wander through life giving little or no thought to the underpinnings of their personal happiness.

Clarifying values and articulating value-aligning activities will make an enormous difference in finding your true greatness—your sources of joy in life.

Failure to link your goals and values increases the risk that you will focus on jackrabbits—work toward goals unrelated to your personal values. Such goals are hollow and provide little lasting satisfaction.

As we near the end of our discussion of goals, I want to share one idea with you. This thought is seldom mentioned in self-help literature. It's . . .

The Dark Side of Setting Goals

Goals are powerful either as tools or weapons. Focusing our goals inevitably causes them to come to pass. But the gypsy curse also comes to mind: "May you get all you wish for."

A *curse*, you say? It is the nature of many of us to wish for some things that may not be good for us. Often, this problem of unwise goals arises from being too self-centered.

Self-centeredness also appears too frequently in books and tapes promoting "success." Many people experience frustration because their goals are all self-centered. Real success and life satisfaction come from setting and attaining objectives that can serve the mutual needs and desires of other people—what Denis Waitley calls the "double-win."

"In our status-oriented culture," Waitley explains, "winning at the expense of others is more important than winning by sharing with and caring for others." He goes on to say that "Today's 'winning-warp' has caused me to see that like any good thing, winning can become twisted and perverted."[3]

But a change is occurring that Waitley sees as the basis for a better world: "I see a painful metamorphosis taking place in society that is every bit as dramatic as the magic transformation of the caterpillar into a butterfly. The very nature of winning is in transition. Our former basis for defining winning, according to external standards set by a hedonistic, egocentric, highly impressionable society, is being transformed. The new view of winning is based on *internal* standards which, while differing for each individual, are consistent in that they take into account moral and spiritual values and principles that affect all of humankind and the natural world."[4]

What is the "double win?" Simply stated: "If I help you win, I win, too." People who take that idea to heart and pattern their actions after it today will be the heroes of tomorrow.

---

[3]Denis Waitley, *The Double Win*, 1985, p. 23.
[4]*Ibid.* p. 30.

The dark side of goal setting? Self-centeredness to the exclusion of others. This can be overcome by thinking "win-win." As you work through the process of goal setting, you'll be much happier if you consider the feelings and needs of other people. It often makes sense to discuss with your spouse, family, or significant others the direction you've chosen for your new life. Often, you'll find that as you consider their needs, they'll help you to achieve what you seek.

Behaviors that Help Anchor Your Values
(☑ Check those behaviors you've tried)

☐ 1. To apply the ideas presented in this chapter, review and work through the activities described. Regularly review your values, redefining them as necessary.

☐ 2. For each core value you identified in Chapter 2, complete a Life Plan worksheet by writing several action targets to help you achieve congruence with each value. Formalize your commitment to value congruence by typing or carefully printing your values and related activities on Life Plan forms or similar sheets. Carry these sheets with you and discipline yourself to review them regularly, especially as you set monthly, weekly, or daily goals. Use the power of values to achieve and maintain your focus.

☐ 3. Schedule a periodic review of your values. Write in your planner or on your calendar a specific time when you will have a personal strategic planning session, reviewing and modifying your values as needed. I'd suggest a quarterly or semi-annual review. After the review, neatly write out your values. (Although this may seem repetitious, writing helps program the brain and can do no harm.)

☐ 4. Double check your goals and values to see if they are excessively self-centered. If they are, rethink them in terms of the "double-win." How can you win by helping someone else win? Jot down specific ideas.

☐ 5. Write a detailed description of your "ideal day." What, exactly, will your life be like when you have achieved your current goals and value congruence? Take all the senses into account. What will you do? How will you feel? How will it look, sound, taste, smell?

CHAPTER 4

TAKE—AND KEEP CONTROL OF YOUR LIFE _____

> *There are uncontrollable elements in everyone's life. It saves a lot of time to recognize these and accept them. Wishing they didn't exist is not a good use of one's time.*
> —Author

> *If you cannot control time, there's only one thing you can control in relation to time—the way you spend your time!*
> —Nido R. Qubein

The two stages of *Best Idea #2: Do the Right Things*—value clarification and self-mastery—are powerful tools for focusing your efforts toward success. A third "right thing" will be discussed in this chapter: gaining and maintaining *control.*

Without a realistic sense of what can or cannot be controlled, we are destined to a life of wasted effort and ineffective results. If we disperse our time and energy on the uncontrollable, we waste precious resources. If, instead, we adapt to circumstances beyond our control and apply our energies over those things we can control, we will be tremendously productive.

Do the following stories sound familiar?

Jerry was excited about this particular Saturday. He had had a rough week, and it was going to feel good to just kick back and do a few odd jobs around the house. Then maybe he could catch the baseball game on TV. His plan started unraveling almost immediately.

After jogging a few miles, Jerry was ready for breakfast but there was no coffee. "I'll just run down to Gas & Go and get some," he thought. So off he went to the convenience store when the left rear tire on the Chevy blew out. "Not to worry," he thought, "I'll pop on the spare and be on my way. Nothing is going to ruin this day." But the spare was flat, too, and Jerry found himself driving on the rim for the two blocks back to the house.

No sooner had he finished his breakfast minus his cup of coffee, when his wife, Meg, reminded him of their appointment for a family photo to be taken at 12:30. "And Tommy has to have a haircut *before* then," she reminded him. "He looks like a six-year-old punk rocker. He hates getting his hair cut, so you'd better take him. Since we're down to one car and I need to get some groceries, I'll drop you off at the barber shop and come back for you in an hour." Meg had it all figured out.

Unfortunately, the lines at the grocery store were long and one hour turned into almost two. While Jerry sat stewing and trying to entertain an active, ex-punker six-year-old, he remembered that he was supposed to call the guys about the change in the bowling team meeting next Monday. He'd better reach Hank and Wally before they went out fishing tomorrow morning, or he'd never catch them. "Is there a pay phone around here?" he asked the girl at the barber shop. Finding the phone, he realized he had no change. He couldn't remember either fellow's phone number, and the phone directory had been shredded beyond recognition. "I should have written those numbers down on something," he swore to himself.

The rest of the day didn't go much better. The photographer was running behind schedule and the portrait was lousy. Jerry finally got Hank's wife on the phone; she offered to pass on the message to Wally. Jerry missed the ball game on TV—but the Cubs lost anyhow. It wasn't until Monday morning when he left for work that he remembered his flat tire on the Chevy. He was forced to take the bus...

Sound familiar? If not, how about this one: Angela left work at 5:30 p.m. carrying her briefcase containing the Collier report, which she would review once more before going to bed. As she maneuvered her way out of the parking lot, the question uppermost on her mind was what to fix for dinner in the short time between arriving home and leaving again to attend the PTA meeting at the kids' school. She thought to herself...

"I really need to get better organized in planning meals. The family has about had it with TV dinners. That Collier report could really give me some visibility in the department if I present it well. Hey, I'm about due for a raise and maybe a promotion. I wonder if the kids have clean socks to wear tomorrow. Oh, and Erika needs a new pair of shoes. I need to take her shopping. If I can just get some financial projections validated before presenting the Collier report, it would have more impact. The junior high school fundraiser is coming up soon. I really should volunteer to chair it. I wonder if there is enough spaghetti left from last night to feed the kids and Bob. Maybe it'll have to be TV dinners just one more time until I get my act together."

Angela suddenly realized that she was two exits past the off-ramp home. Now she'll be late taking Jamie to his basketball practice, and she'll never make it to the PTA meeting on time.

Just like frazzled Angela and disoriented Jerry, many people feel enormous pressures not only to participate, but to *excel* in dozens of different activities. Never before in history have we been expected to do so much, so well.

No wonder we often see life as a rat race or a killer treadmill. We experience a terrible lack of control—a compulsion to move, without form or reason, simply because the rest of the world is whirling around us. And it is this sense of being controlled that creates personal disharmony, disappointment, and unhappiness. Unfortunately, surrendering to external controlling elements makes it virtually impossible for us to bounce back.

Just how do we step gracefully off the treadmill or decline to run a particular rat race? By accepting two critically important facts:

1. We can take charge of our own lives!

and

2. We are 100 percent responsible for what happens in our lives.

You may not be convinced of the validity of these two ideas right now, but I'm going to try to convince you that these facts are absolutely true and that we gain power to bounce back by accepting them. Read on, and you'll see what I mean.

Who *Is* In Charge Here?

There are things we can—and must—do to gain control, take charge, "own" our success, break through our control hangups, and *be far happier than we have ever been before.*

First, we must take responsibility for creating a positive mindset. Our mindset is determined by two things:

1. Our physical state at a given moment, and
2. How we perceive the world

Our physical state is determined by a range of physiological conditions: whether we are tired or alert, happy or grouchy, physically fit or impaired, standing straight or slouching, etc.

If we are tired, grouchy, and slumped in a chair, it's virtually impossible to feel enthusiastic. If we are smiling and dancing with joy, it's impossible to be depressed. Your mental state cannot contradict your physical state. If you doubt this, try the following: Raise your hands above your head, jump up and down like a triumphant boxer and say, "I'm depressed." It doesn't work.

How we perceive the world is determined by three things: positive or negative orientation, perception of control, and language use.

Do you tend to look at the reasons something cannot work before considering why it might work? Is your first reaction to an idea generally positive or negative? Do you dread new experiences or assume they'll be good? These may be indicators of whether you hold a positive sensory orientation (PSO) or a negative sensory orientation (NSO). PSO people are generally optimistic, assuming the best from life. NSO people look to the dark side and can supply all kinds of reasons why something won't work.

Our perception of control also affects our mindset. It has been said that "Whether you feel that you control your life or that your life is controlled by external forces that you have little affect on, you are right." If you are convinced that you are merely a victim of some larger forces over which you have no control, you will, in fact, forfeit your control. Your fantasy becomes a hopeless reality.

If you know that you do in fact have a great deal of control over your own destiny, this, too, becomes a reality for you.

Finally, the way we use language to describe the world we experience determines our mindset. As discussed in Chapter 1, people with a simplistic, either-or, black-white perception of the world are most unhappy. The world has many areas and if the language we use forces us into simplistic thinking, we will have an unrealistic picture of the world. It is impossible to exert control when our underlying assumptions are oversimplified and incorrect.

We Are Responsible for Our Own Lives

We bounce back from adversity when we accept 100 percent responsibility for the *control* and *direction* of our lives. Both are linked; they cannot work independently. We decide our attitude toward, and ability to, control our lives. We also decide how we'll use that power of control to give direction to our lives. We develop a guidance system that is unique for our personal journey.

TRY THIS: Direction and Control Self-Quiz

Check yes or no beside each of the following statements to indicate how you act *as a general rule.* Apply the statement to your life in general, not just on the job. Self-evaluations work best when you answer candidly. Don't write what you think *should be* true; write what *really is.*

1. ☐ yes ☐ no   I spend most of my day doing what other people want me to do.
2. ☐ yes ☐ no   I wait until deadlines are near before I really get going on a project.
3. ☐ yes ☐ no   I work on the "squeaky wheel" principle: the task, person, or thing that "makes the most noise" gets worked on first.
4. ☐ yes ☐ no   I normally wait for someone to tell me what to do.
5. ☐ yes ☐ no   I have a clear picture of where I am going with my professional life during the next five years.
6. ☐ yes ☐ no   People I trust and count on for support (family, close friends, work associates) know my professional plans.
7. ☐ yes ☐ no   I have specific targets for my personal life during the next five years.
8. ☐ yes ☐ no   The values that shape and influence my life decisions are sharp and clear in my mind.
9. ☐ yes ☐ no   I write down my plans, values, and goals.
10. ☐ yes ☐ no   I am satisfied with the progress I am making toward my professional and personal life goals.
11. ☐ yes ☐ no   Sometimes I feel guilty about the successes I have had.
12. ☐ yes ☐ no   I am as successful as I can expect to be at this point in my life.

So What Does this Self-Quiz Mean?

The questions above are designed to start you thinking about several ideas that relate very closely to life control and self-management.

Items 1 through 4 focus on your **attitude toward control.** If you answered "yes" to two or more of these, you probably feel that you must **react** to the world around you. You have probably developed habits of bouncing off the demands of people, situations, or things that seem to be controlling you. You have undoubtedly forfeited much of the control you have a right to retain. In a sense, you have become a slave to the immediate, a servant to all. You have lost (or never asserted) control over your life. It's time to regain the reins before this horse gallops off into The Land of the Haphazard.

Items 5 through 9 reflect your **attitudes toward focus and direction** in your life. If you answered "no" to two or more of these questions, you have probably not given sufficient effort to goal setting. It's time to take another look at *written goals* based on *clarified values.* These provide your most powerful source of energy for propelling you toward success.

Items 10 through 12 focus on your **attitudes toward success.** Each of us has our own perception of what we realistically can hope to accomplish in life. Usually, we're wrong. Most of us don't allow ourselves to dream the big dream. Why? Because we accept others' advice about the limits we *ought to* place on ourselves. We carry around psychological baggage others have dropped on us along the way. It's stuff we don't need, because it encourages us to think small.

Thinking small creates another bind: if we exceed our self-defined limits, often we feel guilty. Guilt engendered by success is a major problem for a surprisingly large number of people. By setting goals too low, we make our comfort zone too small. Then, when we exceed our predictions, we experience discomfort instead of joy.

A Healthy Passion for Control

The quiz on the previous page should give you some ideas on the degree to which you are in control of your life and destiny. Gaining additional control over the factors that influence your life is a continuing process. The more effectively you exert control over that which can be controlled, the better your life will be.

Sometimes from an appreciation for being in control grows from a situation of being out of control. Perhaps you've had an experience something like this:

Mindy remembers well the first time she went skiing. She was with her husband Tom, both newcomers to the sport. With a neighbor couple, they visited a beautiful Utah ski resort. After slipping around and generally looking klutzy as their friends Dave and Judy explained the basics (like how to stand on the skis and how to create the illusion that they've done all this before), they positioned themselves for a ride up the lift.

It took only a few minutes on the lift for a terrifying thought to enter Mindy's mind. She noticed that the lift seats were coming back down the mountain—empty. She also deduced that the lift didn't seem to stop to let people off. That meant that they were going to have to *ski* off the top of the mountain—to certain death, she was sure.

That, friends, is a feeling of having *no* control. And although Mindy and Tom actually became pretty good skiers, they will never forget that first lift-ride-to-certain-death!

Kids may risk forfeiting their control—sometimes. They eagerly take such chances as trying *every* ride at the amusement park. The more threatening the name of the ride, the greater its appeal. The Maniacal Rodent, Terror Mountain, The Bone Crusher—they love 'em all.

But for most adults most of the time, rationality prevails and senseless risk-taking is usually avoided.

While we may miss out on some fun in our old age, one factor underlies our conservative tendency: we really do want to stay in *control*. As grownups, we rebel against the feeling that we lack control of our lives. Why put ourselves into a situation over which we have no control? The more control we can assert, the better. After all, life is unpredictable enough in its natural course.

An experience from my youth fired me with a passion for control. My buddy, John, a friend from a town about 20 miles away, rode past my house one summer afternoon in a pretty neat Ford convertible driven by Stan. I didn't know Stan, but John insisted that I hop in and ride with them.

After an hour of cruising, Stan decided to go home. He lived next door to John. Unfortunately, Stan didn't feel any particular obligation to return me to my house. So there I was, dropped off 20 miles from home with darkness coming on.

I remember my helpless feeling as I hitchhiked home. And I vowed that I'd never let myself get into such a situation again. To this day, I almost always volunteer to drive when going out with other people. I just like to maintain control.

Despite wanting to be more in control, that out-of-control feeling becomes more common as life becomes more complicated. The stories of Angela and Jerry are fairly typical of the juggling acts people perform. Career, family, civic or religious activity, physical fitness, school, and self-improvement all take a bite out of our precious time and drain our limited energy. This, coupled with a "do-more, do-better" mind set, places a lot of pressure on people. And as with a runaway truck, a crash is inevitable unless we put on the brakes—or at least steer the thing.

So, how do we get in control? First, we need a realistic picture of the process of controlling. With a clearer mindset we go a long way toward learning how to get off that ski lift, not by jumping into space, but by negotiating our way downhill. Climb aboard.

Free at Last!

The time of our lives is measured by the *events* or activities that take place. If nothing ever happened, time would be irrelevant. If we are doing *nothing,* there are no deadlines. How we use time matters very much, however, when we choose to do *something.* "Life-control" means controlling our activities. Most of us have plenty to choose from! The trick is to manage life rather than let life manage us.

Some of the *events* or activities we choose from are momentous; many are small and insignificant. Getting married, starting a new career, having children, and purchasing a home are major events. Likewise, big events we didn't choose, like war, economic crash, extreme weather, or a presidential election, may well affect our lives.

But life is also an endless stream of little activities such as completing routine projects, handling daily activities, spending time with friends, attending seminars, or simply doing the dishes.

The question is, "Just how much control do I really have over all these activities and events?"

TRY THIS:

Think for a moment about some of the many events that affect your life. Big events or little tasks, it doesn't matter. In the space below you'll see three vertical columns. From left to right label these columns, "No Control," "Gray Area," and "Much Control."

First, in the left column, list some events over which you have *NO* control. Then, in the right column of the sheet, list some events over which you have a *GREAT DEAL* of control. Don't belabor this, but just list five or six of each type. (We'll come back to the "gray area" in a moment.)

No Control	Gray Area	Much Control
_____	_____	_____
_____	_____	_____
_____	_____	_____
_____	_____	_____
_____	_____	_____
_____	_____	_____
_____	_____	_____
_____	_____	_____

Now that you have listed some events you can control and others you cannot, let's examine our attitudes toward the whole process of control.

Attitudes Toward Control

Some people see the world as one in which they have almost no freedom to manage their own lives. Their mindset is externally directed. These people live in a pinball machine world, bouncing off the demands of other people, events, and obligations.

To them, it seems futile to try to manage their lives. They leave their fate to chance. There is a name for people who don't manage their own lives. They are "unsuccessful."

The flip side of their attitude is *never* to react to others. That would be impossible and undesirable. To some extent, we are all reactive to outside demands. For eight hours a day we go to work and do what our boss wants. We commit ourselves to family, civic work, church activity, and the like, and by doing so, forfeit the option of doing what we feel like doing at the moment. We may cooperate with others for some larger good.

This need to contribute to cooperative efforts has been around ever since the cave man first asked the guy in the next cave to help him move a boulder. Without such cooperation, humanity would have been limited to accomplishing no more than what one person working alone could do. And that isn't much.

We could call such cooperative activities *donated* time. Just as in giving money to our favorite charity, we give away control over how our money will be used, so is it with our time. Once our time is donated, we give up our control over that chunk of time. So long as something worthwhile comes of it, we're pleased with our donation. Nevertheless, some people get so bogged down in obligations, they never get around to doing what's *important to them* as individuals.

Occasionally, we need to take a hard look at the quantity and quality of our donated time and see if it is really productive and gratifying.

Remember, your donated time is voluntary. You can take back control if you reclaim the time, although you may well pay, as the bankers say, "a substantial penalty for early withdrawal." Penalties can include incurring the anger of others or feeling guilty. Nevertheless, if the cost isn't too much to swallow, cutting back on such obligations is a logical option.

The activities over which we have much control (in the right column) are *flexible actions.* As the term implies, time used for these activities is discretionary. It's the time we have left after the donated hours are spent. Much of the good we accomplish in life will result from what we do with our discretionary time.

What's Lurking in the Gray Area

Between what we can control and what we can't, there is a large gray area. In that gray area dwells all we can *partially* control or influence. Also, within the gray area lurks two misperceptions that can cause people to accomplish less and feel frustrated. These are:

1. Programmed limitations, and
2. Illusions of control

Write those two phrases in the "gray area" (center) column on your list of events on page 93.

The Pesky Problem of Programmed Limitations

Our brain is constantly being programmed as to what we can or cannot do. By experience, we learn our limitations. But sometimes these limits are not valid—some hacker input bad data into our system. Too often, our operating system reflects someone else's ideas about our limitations. How can others know our limitations? *We* aren't even sure about them ourselves.

A bad childhood experience can cause us to sell ourselves short when there is no logical reason to do so. The kid who isn't picked when sides are chosen for a playground softball game programs her brain: *softball: no good.* In fact, she may have considerable talent but *looks like* a lousy ballplayer to the other kids. A youngster can be scarred for life and discouraged from enjoying an activity all because she just didn't look like a ballplayer to a few other kids.

Another kid is raised in a blue-collar culture that teaches him that he, too, is limited to a future in the factory or mine.

Sometimes, society at large does the programming. A gremlin called COMMON KNOWLEDGE decrees what can or cannot be done. Before 1954, for example, it was COMMON KNOWLEDGE throughout the sporting world that a human being could not run a mile in less than four minutes. That limitation was programmed into the brains of people everywhere, except that of a fellow named Roger Bannister. He must have been living on another planet, because apparently nobody told him about the four minute barrier. Or if they did, he ignored this "fact."

A funny thing happened after Bannister broke through the four-minute mile barrier. Within months, other runners beat his time. Today, sub-four-minute miles are almost commonplace in world-class track events. What happened to the limitation? That accepted truth about what could never be done popped like a soap bubble.

Motivational books today are full of examples of how people overcome limitations to achieve greatness. Maybe, just maybe, your setback or slump is being shored up by some programmed limitations. It make sense to re-examine our supposed limitations to see if they exist only in our minds.

TRY THIS: Always Ask, "Is this Barrier Real?"

The starting point for overcoming barriers and bouncing back from failures (real or imagined) is to determine if the barrier exists in reality or only in our minds. Take a moment and list some of the barriers that stand between you and what you really want from life. Jot down any kinds of barriers that come to mind: physical, mental, educational, financial, or social.

Next, ask yourself this hard question for each barrier:

Is it possible—just possible—that this barrier is an invalid limitation I have accepted as real? If it is, or could be, act as if it is only a mirage. Now, go after what you really want.

My barriers	Why is this barrier real? Could it be artificial or imagined?
_____	_____
_____	_____
_____	_____

Dream On: Illusions Of Control

Now, let's investigate the opposite of the programmed limitation: the *illusion of control.* Some things in life *are* beyond personal control, some limitations *are* real. When I ask people in seminars to name some things that really *cannot* be controlled, they typically identify the weather, death, and taxes, the stock market, household pets, and teenagers. I'm not so sure about pets and teenagers, but I'd generally agree with the first items listed.

When you really can't control an event, the appropriate response is to *adapt* to it. Don't get yourself into a self-defeating dither over events you cannot control.

And of all the uncontrollables in life, other people are the ones you'll run into most often. You can attempt to influence, manipulate, persuade, cajole, intimidate, or plead with other people. But you can not *control* them. Be aware of this genuine limitation.

Most of the time, people are motivated by self-interest. If your attempt to control them isn't in line with what they want to do, you're not likely to prevail—unless you have a lot of power. This isn't to say that we should never attempt to control the behaviors of others. Just make the attempt with your eyes open: Your chances of success are often slim.

Periodically ask yourself, "Do I really have control, or should I sometimes let go and simply adapt?"

If the weather is bad, carry an umbrella or wear a hat. Don't get all bent out of shape about it. If the market is down, hold for the long term or get out, whichever is more comfortable for you. If you absolutely cannot get along with someone despite your best efforts, stay away from the jerk.

And when you've decided what to do, *never look back.* It'll do you no good—the past is beyond your control. Only today—right now!—can be controlled.

"Control" Is a Relative Term

Can we really manage our lives or must we just adapt to what someone told us is uncontrollable? Isn't control really a relative term? I think it is. Here's a scenario that makes the point:

Suppose you were told that if you come to a particular office in a city 50 miles away at exactly 3 o'clock you would be given a check for $100,000, tax free. It's yours to keep.

You say you don't have a car? I bet you'd find transportation. But suppose a truck has overturned and the freeway is blocked five miles from your destination? You must be there in 45 minutes, but you are stuck in gridlock. Would you submit to this unfortunate turn of events, shrug your shoulders, sigh "what will be will be," and give up the money? I seriously doubt it. (People like that don't read books like this!)

You'd not let anything stand in your way, wouldn't you? You'd jog the last five miles, commandeer a bicycle, or steal a pogo stick—but you'd get there.

You'd *take control* because the reward for doing so is sufficiently compelling.

We can overcome all sorts of limitations if we really want to. Just as the obstacles on the highway can be overcome, so can programmed limitations, as long as we know where we are going and have a burning desire to get there. Don't let programmed limitations hold you back from getting what you're after. Tell the world to "listen to the sound of my wheels" as you take off, in control, and reach your goals.

Keep a Realistic Perspective

Be realistic about the way things are but don't fail to dream the bigger dream. You can overcome the kinds of problems that may be frustrating you by first looking hard at reality and then determining what strings can be pulled to shape your own world.

The bedrock upon which the super-successful person can best build his or her life is *control*. Without it, there is no chance of success. With a realistic perspective on control, all things are possible. Understand control, seek control, and know when to let go of control.

Specific Behaviors that Help You Get in the Habit of Being in Control
(☑ Check off when you've completed each item)

☐ 1. To apply the ideas discussed in this chapter, start now by expanding the lists of activities or events you can and cannot control. Select one item from the list of those you feel you can control but that you are not now controlling as effectively as you might. Now, write out a description of what actions you will take to control that item better.

Susan shared this example: She listed "exercise time" as an activity within her control but not optimally controlled. Susan liked to walk 30 minutes every evening right after work, but when family members needed her to run errands for them, she often used her exercise time to accommodate them. Here's what she did: She explained to her family why exercising was important to her. Then she told them what times she would be available to help them. Finally, she stuck to her commitment to herself with her family's cooperation.

☐ 2. Next, review the items on your noncontrollable list. Assess each item to see if it *really* is beyond your control. Select one item that you might actually have some control over and write out how you might take additional control.

☐ 3. Look again at the items you put in the noncontrollable list. Select one item from that list and describe a plan for *adapting* to it so that you can comfortably put it behind you and move on.

☐ 4. When in doubt as to whether you should spend some of your control on an activity someone else wants you to do, ask:

- Am I being too quick to *react* to the needs of others?
- Should my own priorities take precedence over what is being asked of me?
- Is the requested action worthy of my precious donated time?
- Is this the best possible use of my time and effort in light of my goals and values?

Develop the habit of answering these questions before donating your time and effort.

☐ 5. Practice the art of adapting. When faced with a situation you simply cannot control, do your best to adapt to it and tough it out without amplifying the pain. Grin and bear it, for this too shall pass. All things do.

☐ 6. Learn to anticipate the effects of your actions on your ability to maintain control. Are you doing everything possible to maintain control? Are you going to be stuck without a ride home? Is there anything else you can do to maintain control? By agreeing to do X, will you lose control over Y? Will agreement to do X obligate you to continue to do it even if you don't want to later?

☐ 7. Think back on an example where you felt completely in control. Recall the situation vividly. Amplify it in your mind. Make the picture bright, the sounds loud and clear. Remember how it felt. Now, hold that image and apply it to a current situation.

BEST IDEA 3

Do Things Right

CHAPTER 5

TAPPING YOUR MENTAL POWER SOURCES _____

> *I was going to buy a copy of* The Power of Positive
> Thinking, *and then I thought: What the hell good would
> that do?*
>
> —Ronnie Shakes

> *What you think about expands [into action, reality]. I
> never think about what I don't want to expand.*
>
> —Dr. Wayne Dyer

Take a look around you. Now, pause to think that everything you see was created mentally before it was created physically. Your home, furniture, office, that cup of coffee, the eyeglasses you are looking through, automobiles, clothing—everything you see started out as an idea, as a thought.

No one in his right mind would begin to create something without thinking it through first. So when it comes to building a strategy for bouncing back from slumps or setbacks, we, too, must first go to our minds—our mental power source.

Isn't it amazing to think that all that we are physically lay in that tiny drop of protoplasm that began our life. All our physical characteristics— the color of our eyes, hair, and skin, our build, and our facial features—all are there from the instant we are conceived.

It's the same way with the mind. We bring to this life a mental capacity to solve any problem we will ever face, to create anything we can vividly imagine, and to answer our most pressing questions. We just need to learn how to tap our intelligence.

The great motivational speaker Zig Ziglar once told me that there are three principles he always mentions when speaking to people:

1. You are what and where you are because of what goes on in your mind.
2. The past is never as important as how you see the future, and
3. If there's faith in your future, there's power in your future.

The human mind is extraordinarily powerful. We often compare the mind with a sophisticated data processor. But it can do what even today's most sophisticated computers cannot. Its special power lies not in crunching numbers or processing words but in its ability to generate thought—to create! The mind is the source of all success.

You've heard that even the brightest people use only a small percentage of their mental abilities. In fact, recent studies suggest that we use even less than was originally thought, perhaps only two or three percent of our capacity.

You'll See It When You Believe It

Exciting breakthroughs occur for those who learn to tap more of their mind's potential. To do so, we must first accept the premise that all things are created mentally before they can come about physically. Likewise, that which can be conceived in the mind can become reality. As Dr. Wayne Dyer says, "You'll see it [in reality] when you believe it [mentally]."

The skills necessary to create a new mental world are not difficult to learn, although they have often been shrouded in mystery. In this chapter, we will explore three ways to tap our unconscious. The first is through *imaging* or *self-hypnosis*. The second is through *modeling* or *mental rehearsals*. The third is through *subliminal programming*.

All three of these approaches may work very effectively for you, or perhaps only one or two will produce the results you want. But each is potentially useful, so approach each with the assumption that it will be. Don't fight it with skepticism. Assume it will work, and it most likely will.

Imaging or Self-Hypnosis

Some people prefer the terms "imaging" or "visualization" or "envisioning." Others like "self-hypnosis," "guided imagery," or "meditation." Choose the term you like best; all are processes for tapping your subconscious powers.

Hypnosis is frequently misunderstood. When stage magicians employ the technique, people may do or say unusual things. People fear embarrassment or loss of control if they succumb to hypnosis. Nothing, however, could be further from the truth. Let's first clear up some of the myths and see what hypnosis really is.

What Is Hypnosis or Imaging?

One of the most common myths about hypnosis is that someone takes control of your mind. This is not true. No one can be hypnotized if he or she does not wish to be, and you cannot be made to do anything in hypnosis that would be contrary to your values.

In reality, there is nothing mysterious or magical about hypnosis.

> *Hypnosis is simply a state of concentration and focused attention.*

Hypnosis, or imaging, is a perfectly natural state of consciousness. For example, think of times you have been driving down a road, deep in thought. Suddenly you "snap out of it," realizing that for several blocks you haven't seen anything you've passed. You were inwardly absorbed, focused in such a way that you weren't even aware that you were driving.

Fortunately, your unconscious mind, programmed with many of hours of driving experience, was running on auto-pilot. Your subconscious said, "Leave the driving to us."

Similarly, when we are engrossed in a good movie, play, TV show, book, or some task that we are really enjoying, World War III could break out and we wouldn't even notice! Focused, concentrated states of attention are naturally occurring hypnotic or trance-like states. The trick is to *use* these as a means for self-direction, to help us program our future in a systematic and constructive way.

How Hypnosis Puts Your Mind to Work

As with any other skill, systematically tapping into our underlying mental powers takes practice. A good starting point is simply to recognize that our imaginations contain billions of bits of useful information.

Through self-hypnosis, we focus our imagination and thought processes on creating feelings that, in turn, alter our attitudes and behaviors. With imaging, first we change our internal world. Changes in the external world must inevitably follow.

If you ever talked to your boss about a well-deserved raise, you probably first rehearsed the conversation mentally. Similarly, imaging focuses a state of attention and concentration that allows us to rehearse what is to be. Imaging is reality in the making.

Of the six steps to successful self-hypnosis, we have already discussed the first: Believe in its potential. The other five are:

- Schedule practice time
- Set objectives for each imaging session
- Induce a state of focused concentration
- Introduce hypnotic suggestions
- Introduce post-hypnotic suggestions

Scheduling Practice Time

Initially, it's helpful to practice self-hypnosis in a quiet place where you will be undisturbed. As you become more proficient, you will be able to hypnotise yourself effectively in almost any setting.

In preparation, take the phone off the hook, post a "do not disturb" sign, and request that others not interrupt you. You may want to dim the lights. Sit in a comfortable, high-back chair that will support your neck. This is usually better than lying down because most of us have a conditioned response to drift off to sleep when lying down. Sit so that your legs are not crossed and your hands not touching.

Plan to spend 20–30 minutes for practice, particularly at first. Later, you may be able to enter a hypnotic state more quickly. Of course, the amount of time spent may depend on the complexity of the problem or goals on which you're working.

Set aside a regular time for imaging, preferably on a daily basis. Give it a high priority, for it will pay tremendous dividends.

Imaging, however, is not a substitute for consciously addressing your goals or challenges. Use your conscious mind to the fullest as you work your plan for success. But then, discipline yourself to set aside time to tune in to your unconscious inner resources. Don't expect the unconscious to solve all your problems or achieve all your goals for you. Your sustained effort is critical to success.

One other word of caution: Be patient. Some people can pick up the benefits of imaging quickly, but others must practice imaging for some time before it bears fruit. Try it for at least 21 days before you pass judgment on its effectiveness.

Set Objectives for Each Imaging Session

TRY THIS: **Write Down Your Goal**

For each imaging session, pinpoint your objective for that session. It's best to concentrate on one or two targets for each imaging experience. Write down the question or issue you would like to resolve or the feelings you'd like to gain before you induce a trance.

Examples:

- "I want to reassure myself that I can find a new and better job and get fresh ideas for where to look."
- "I want to feel more comfortable about my ability to handle my upcoming presentation."
- "I want to get new ideas for marketing our new line of wigits."
- "I want a better understanding of how to strengthen my relationship with my spouse and children."
- "I want to learn to relax and handle stress better."

Add some target areas you'd like to address by tapping your unconscious mind.

Induce a State of Focused Concentration

Inducing a hypnotic state

Many professionals argue that the most effective way to learn to induce self-hypnosis is to train with a psychologist or mental health professional. Seeking professional help is fine. I have found, however, that the process is not all that mysterious. You can learn to induce a hypnotic state quite easily on your own.

The key is to be relaxed. Close your eyes and imagine that your body is going totally limp. One way is to visualize your muscles becoming loose and saggy. Another is to imagine warm water flowing over your feet at first and then rising over your knees, thighs, chest, etc., until you feel almost fluid yourself.

One hypnotist I know suggests that we "picture the color of relaxation. Then see that color flowing down from the top of your head to your toes, slowly soothing as it flows."

A simpler induction might be simply to count as you breathe, starting at 300 and counting backwards, all the time telling yourself to relax.

Deepening your hypnotic state

Once you have induced relaxation, it is important to take some time to deepen your hypnotic state. There are several popular methods for deepening your involvement. You may want to imagine walking gradually down a staircase of 10 or 20 steps, feeling yourself going deeper into a relaxed, focused state with each step. Some people enjoy imagining that they are descending a long escalator or riding in a slow-moving freight elevator.

Progressive relaxation is another useful method. In this method, you imagine relaxation flowing from one part of your body to another. Many people find it helpful to imagine what the muscles would look like, softening, loosening, and becoming deeply relaxed.

Another procedure for deepening the hypnotic state is to imagine peaceful and interesting places or experiences. This may include imagining yourself on the beach, fishing on a lake, camping or hiking in the mountains, floating in a swimming pool, hang gliding, visiting a previous vacation spot, skiing, sailing, listening to a symphony, boating, playing golf, ice skating, playing a musical instrument, watching a sunset, or listening to favorite music. Whatever interests, absorbs, or seems peaceful to you can become your focus. You may find, in fact, that simply visualizing yourself lying back, relaxing very deeply, can deepen your hypnosis.

TRY THIS: Going to Your Special Place

Think back to a time when you were particularly relaxed and serene. Now sharpen the vision of that place. What did it look like? How did it feel, sound, smell? Close your eyes and imagine this special place and make it your mental hideaway—a place where you can go and feel terrific.

(If you can't think of a place you know, *create* an imaginary place—an *ideal* hideaway.)

Now, when you try imaging, go to your special place and re-experience the good feelings.

Describe your place here:

You can learn to allow various aspects of images to become vehicles for taking you deeper into comfort. For example, you may think to yourself, "with each wave that washes up onto the beach, I drift deeper and deeper into relaxation." As an alternative, you might also imagine that each wave is washing away your tension, or that the warmth of the sun is softening and loosening your muscles.

Make your mental scenes as vivid as possible, imagining any details that make it more real for you. If you are imagining yourself on the beach, for instance, imagine the feel of the cool, firm, wet sand. Notice interesting objects in the sand, the smell of the ocean, the warmth of the sun, and the sound of gulls. The details that you elaborate may take the form of sights, sounds, textures, temperatures, emotions, smells, and even tastes. Most of us find it difficult to imagine details in all of these sensory dimensions, but you can rely on the modalities that are most easy for you to create in your mind.

Another technique is called "breathing and counting." Begin by slowly taking five very deep breaths. As you expel each breath, say to yourself, "deeper and deeper" and imagine yourself sinking deeper into relaxation and comfort. After letting out the fifth breath, take another very deep breath, and hold it for a significant length of time (30-40 seconds). Suggest to yourself that "as I let this breath out, I will sag limply back into the chair, and go much, much deeper into a hypnotic state." When you are ready to exhale, let the breath out quickly.

Whenever possible, take 10-20 minutes for deepening hypnosis before you begin giving yourself suggestions.

It is not unusual to become distracted while performing self-hypnosis. A loud noise from another room may startle you, or someone may walk into the room. Or you may feel an itch or the need to shift your body. Feel free to shift your posture or scratch your arm. Once the distraction has passed, you can just take another very deep breath, and return to drifting deeper into a hypnotic state.

At other times, persistent background noises may be disturbing. Sounds of cars driving past, the noise of a furnace or air conditioner, footsteps in the hall, the sound of typing, and the pounding of a jackhammer are all distracting.

There are two ways to utilize persistent background noises. First, give yourself the suggestion that with each sound (e.g., each blow of the jackhammer or whoosh of each passing car) you will descend deeper and deeper into your trance. In this manner, the sounds themselves are converted into deepening modalities. A second way to use distracting sounds is to imagine that they are in some way associated with the pleasant imagery that you are using. For instance, if you are imagining yourself on the beach, the sound of children outside your window can become the sound of children playing on the beach. You might "translate" the sound of the air conditioner into the sound of waves or the wind in palm trees.

Don't become overly preoccupied or worried about how well you are doing. Just allow things to happen the way they seem to want to happen. Learn to trust the wisdom deep inside of you, and allow the imagery to evolve spontaneously. If you are not entirely sure that you are hypnotized, go ahead and use your imagination anyway, assuming that you are hynotized. It may be that your notion of hypnosis is unrealistic—so don't wait for it to happen.

Introducing Hypnotic Suggestions

Writing out your goals or hypnotic suggestions before an imaging session helps you focus on your subconscious. Now, here's a way to benefit even more from your imaging:

TRY THIS: **Taped Hypnotic Suggestions**

Tape record your suggestions before inducing a trance. Talk slowly, with a relaxed, confident tone of voice. In preparing the tapes, experiment to see if you prefer hearing the suggestions in the first person ("I am . . .") or in the second person ("You are . . ."), as if someone else were speaking to you.

I like to use a tape player with a headset. I have the player in my lap. Then, once I've induced a relaxed state, I simply switch on my prerecorded messages.

If no tape recorder is available, simply repeat your hypnotic suggestions to yourself when you are deeply relaxed.

Your hypnotic suggestions work best when phrased positively. As you write or speak your suggestions, avoid words like "don't," "won't," "can't," "shouldn't," "try," "no," and "not." Instead, use positive phrases with strong verbs such as: "I earn," "I build," "I can," "I will find," "I am free from," and "I have mastered."

Words like "always" and "never" should be avoided in most hypnotic suggestions. If, for example, our goal is to lose 20 pounds, and we say, "I will *never* eat desserts again," we are probably setting ourselves up for failure. Likewise, a statement such as, "I will always keep my cool in business meetings," may be unrealistic.

Do not impose time limitations on your suggestions. Saying "I will be calm and cool when I stand up to make a presentation to my customers" expects too much. A better suggestion might be, "As I begin my presentation to a customer, I will begin to feel a sense of calm that will allow me to be relaxed and spontaneous." Avoid demanding or perfectionistic statements. Words like "soon" or "will begin to" avoid imposing unrealistic time limits that make us feel like failures if instantaneous and complete success doesn't occur.

TRY THIS: **Phrasing Hypnotic Suggestions**

List below several hypnotic suggestions you will use as you apply this technique. Check to be sure that they meet the criteria described above.

Introduce Post-hypnotic Suggestions

You can continue to benefit from hypnosis long after coming out of a trance by using "post-hypnotic suggestions." These are thoughts planted in the subconscious while hynotized that will trigger desired reactions later. They are linked to future situations you are bound to face.

For example, while hypnotized, we may program our mind to associate an action (say, hanging our coat up at the office) with a feeling (an enthusiasm for doing an excellent job). We may associate handing a customer a pen with confidence in closing a sale; opening the refrigerator with the feeling of satisfaction that comes from becoming slimmer.

Sometimes we describe a feeling first and then associate an action with it. For example, we may tell our mind that when we feel a craving for a candy bar, we will instead drink a glass of water.

In introducing post-hypnotic suggestions, use the following format: "When I feel (angry, the desire to eat, nervous, a desire for a cigarette), I will take a deep breath, hold it, and as I exhale, feel a sense of calm comfort wash over me." Be specific. For example, if you were suffering from insomnia, you might give yourself the following post-hypnotic suggestion: "As I feel my head touch the pillow (an inevitable action), I will begin to yawn and become very sleepy."

The cues or triggers for post-hypnotic suggestions can be:

1. Inevitable actions or behaviors;
2. Visual cues (e.g., the sight of the refrigerator, a TV commercial, seeing someone light a cigarette);
3. Sounds (e.g., your dog barking, your spouse using a familiar word or expression, the sound of the lunch whistle);
4. Physical feelings, sensations, or smells (e.g., the smell of food or a cigarette, bodily tension, hunger pangs);
5. Thoughts or emotions (e.g., the thought of eating or having a cigarette, feelings of anger, anxiety, or depression).

TRY THIS: Describe Some Post-hypnotic Suggestions

List several post-hypnotic suggestions you might use in your imaging. Listed below are some types of phrases that you may find helpful as models in writing post-hypnotic suggestions:

"When I _____, I will _____."

"After I _____, I can _____."

"While I _____, I can _____."

"As soon as I _____, then I _____."

"As I _____, I can _____."

"As _____ occurs, I will notice _____."

(Note: If the second person, e.g., "you" instead of "I," works better for you, rephrase the suggestions accordingly.)

Length and Repetition of Suggestions

In general, self-hypnosis is most effective when suggestions are relatively brief—only one to three sentences.

Repetition is important. It is recommended that you present the verbal suggestions to yourself three or more times, preferably using language somewhat varied each time, rather than *exactly* the same. It is vitally important to use visual imagery and imagination to accompany all suggestions. *Picture* the desired condition; *feel* it; *taste* it; *smell* it. Such sensory elaboration repeats the suggestion in a different and compelling way.

". . .when willpower (consciously trying to do something) is in conflict with imagination, imagination always wins."
—D. Corydon Hammond, Ph.D.

Let me repeat a point I made earlier in this book: Physical work and creative mental work are best accomplished in opposite ways. When doing physical work, the greater the force applied, the more efficiently the task gets done. When driving nails, the harder you swing the hammer, the faster you drive the nail. When pushing a stalled car, the harder you push, the sooner the car moves.

But in mental tasks, the opposite holds true. The more we wrestle with the problem, the *less* likely we are to come up with the best possible solution. Instead, breakthroughs occur when we have learned to relax and permit our subconscious mind to produce an answer. This is the essence of self-hypnosis: To tap the incredible power of the subconscious to provide the answers we need to accomplish our mental tasks.

Trying too hard—exerting willpower—can actually work against us. Recall a time when you went to bed late and were anxious about having to get up early the next morning. The harder you tried to get to sleep, the more wide awake you felt. Instead of trying to will yourself to sleep, you would have been better off permitting your mind to relax and forgetting about not being able to sleep. If you could have become lost in a peaceful fantasy, your conscious mind would have been occupied with something restful, freeing it from worry about the early morning wakeup time. By occupying the conscious mind, the subconscious could have helped you meet your real goal—getting to sleep. It's likely that sleep would have quickly followed.

My friend Jim used imaging to create his dream of establishing the top real estate dealership in a large southern city.

Each day, Jim set aside 30 minutes for imaging. He retired into a quiet room, where he sat undisturbed in a rather shabby but comfortable chair. Jim would then put himself into a hypnotic state and visualize *exactly* what it would be like when he had reached his goal of becoming the biggest real estate firm in town. He told me that as he imagined his success, he could see *exactly* what his future corporate offices would look like. He saw the furniture, the computers, the employees moving around busily. He heard the voices of his agents as they reported closing another sale, and he could even hear the chalk squeak as the word "sold" was scribbled on the chalkboard. He could smell the leather executive chair, feel the thrill of driving his new Mercedes, observe the looks of admiration as he overheard imaginary people telling others at cocktail parties of "Jim, owner of the largest brokerage in town." Each time Jim imaged his success, the picture grew clearer, the detail more complete, the scene brighter.

And Jim's images became reality!

Using Imaging to Unload Past "Failures"

Experts in neurolinguistic programming (NLP), a rather formidable name for the science of controlling our minds, suggest that we can rid ourselves of fears by dulling the images of them in our mind. More specifically, if we associate our fear or worry with some symbol and then have our mind reduce the vividness of that image, the fear becomes much less formidable.

Say, for example, you have a terrible fear of losing the financial security you have achieved. Seeing your net worth diminish would humiliate and terrify you. Because of this fear, you avoid all risk and feel stymied. You can't even make a business decision for fear of taking a risk.

How could you overcome this? First, associate the fear with some symbol. Any symbol will do. You could choose something logically related, like the old Rambler automobile that you used to own but hated because of its shoddy quality. Or you could choose a cartoon version of your past boss, who chained you to your desk and cracked a whip over your head. The symbol can be anything—and it doesn't have to make sense to anyone else—only to your subconscious mind.

Next, reverse the imaging process I described and *blur* the mental picture. To do so, you may diminish color and brightness, distort size and shape (the Rambler becomes a huge rubbery cartoon car), slow down speed (cracking whip sounds like squeaky chair), or push the whole symbol far into the distance like a computerized TV image that flips away from you.

If your symbolic images of the "dreaded thing" include sounds, turn down the volume. If texture can be associated, make the texture unpleasant, perhaps slimy or exceptionally rough. If the symbol is something soft (like the seats of the Rambler), make them hard like rocks. If you can associate a temperature with the symbol, make it extremely cold or hot.

Some NLP experts suggest picturing your negative symbol as you literally sweep it from your mind, saying aloud the sound "whoosh!" as you whisk it away.

Return to Pleasant Imagery and Awakening

After you have finished your hypnotic work using suggestions and imagery, take a minute or two to relax very deeply with some peaceful imagery. If before you were imaging yourself walking in the mountains working on your problem, you may want to return to the same lovely place and enjoy it for another few moments.

Then, after enjoying a few minutes of deep relaxation, you can gradually awaken yourself. Begin by giving yourself a suggestion for positive feelings after you awake. For instance, "After I awaken, I will feel refreshed, alert, and clear-headed, and I will carry those wonderful feelings with me into the remainder of my day." It is then usually most comfortable to awaken yourself gradually; for instance, by counting slowly backwards from 20 to one.

Modeling Behavior of Others

The second major way we tap the power of the mind is through modeling the behaviors of others. Modeling is essentially imitation in great detail. We see how others handle situations we face, and we try to do the same things. Does modeling make sense? Most psychologists say it does.

If you knew a woman who made the most delicious chocolate cake you ever tasted, could you do the same? Even if she had spent years of trial and error to perfect her recipe, you could duplicate her cake *if you had the exact recipe,* right?

That's exactly the idea behind modeling. We can save years of trial and error if we model someone who is already expert in what we want to do or become. To make our friend's cake, we need:

- the same ingredients
- in the same amounts
- processed in the same order.

Likewise, to duplicate behavioral outcomes, we need to identify the ingredients (usually psychological states or skills developed), replicate the amounts (such as time and effort), and do the same things with these ingredients in the same order.

To learn to bake that cake, we need to watch and measure and replicate carefully. If we do so, we cannot fail to produce an exact replica.

TRY THIS: **Modeling a Behavior**

Think of a behavior you would like to make your own. Identify a model—a person who seems to do this well. Then list as many "ingredients" as he or she seems to use. How does your model process these ingredients to make the outcome you admire?

Your model and what he or she does well.

Ingredients he or she uses to achieve desired results.

How can you duplicate the results of the model?

We can replicate the outcomes of those we admire by modeling. But first, we must identify the people we want to model—people whose results we hope to produce.

Your Council of Advisors

Many years ago, Napoleon Hill wrote the book, *Think and Grow Rich*. This highly successful businessman regularly employed self-hypnotic states. One day he began considering an interesting proposition. If he could somehow have a group of famous people as his personal advisors, whom would he choose? After careful thought, he selected six or seven men from throughout history who possessed different qualities of character that he admired.

Napoleon Hill began putting himself into self-hypnotic states and imagining himself conversing with these famous individuals. Gradually, he seemed to become acquainted with them and they became almost real to him, although he knew that they were only figments of his imagination. Each day for more than 30 years, Mr. Hill entered self-hypnosis and imagined himself going into a boardroom and having a meeting with his personal council of advisors. He consulted with them about both personal and professional matters, finding their contributions invaluable.

There was nothing supernatural about what Napoleon Hill did. There was great wisdom and judgment in his unconscious mind. This method simply gave him a concrete way of accessing that wisdom and in a way that seems perfectly natural to us. Feeling deficient, we are accustomed to asking someone else for answers, even though deep inside we may already know what needs to be done.

> **TRY THIS:**   **Your Council of Advisors**
>
> There are people of wisdom with certain qualities whom you
> would like to have as advisors. They may be people you know,
> religious leaders, or people whose lives you have studied and
> whom you admire.
>
> Make a list of five people you would most like to have as advisors:
>
> 1.
> 2.
> 3.
> 4.
> 5.
>
> Get to know these people personally or vicariously. If they are personal
> friends, get to know them better; if public figures, read about them.
> Then meet these people as you do your imaging. Get acquainted,
> establish a relationship, and then meet regularly with them.

Image a model acting the way you wish to act. The model may be
someone who possesses a desired attribute and whom you know
personally. On the other hand, the model may be someone you know
by reputation or just someone your mind creates. Study this person
noting how he/she handles the situation you anticipate yourself facing.

Next, *visualize yourself* carrying out the suggestions, acting and feeling
differently. Also, and very importantly, *imagine the positive outcomes*
resulting from your change.

This technique is based on the psychological notion called the "act as
if" principle: If you wish to change, *act as if* you were already the way
you wish to be. This behavioral principle is by no means new and is
used by many modern therapists. Most people however, haven't realized
that another principle is equally as important: *think as if.*

As you tap the power of your subconscious mind, *imagine how your
life will be after the changes have already taken place.* Visualize yourself
in the future, after the changes have occurred, and notice what
everything is like and how you feel. This procedure has been called *age
progression.* Imagine that you are drifting ahead in time to a future time

when the changes you desire have already taken place. It may be just a few months in the future or perhaps many years. Notice your new circumstances and *how you naturally act and feel differently.*

From the perspective of this future time, notice all the events that were set in motion because of the original changes that you made previously. In a hypnotic state, you can pretend that you are sitting in a new environment, years in the future, reflecting back on how you used self-hypnosis and changed yourself. And you can appreciate the results of these changes.

Subliminal Programming

The third way to tap the power of our mind is through subliminal programming. The term "subliminal" means below the conscious level. We are not aware of the messages received, yet our mind and body react to them.

This may sound a little spooky, but it's really not. Scientists have long known that we are affected by subconscious messages. Advertising is largely a game of trying to manipulate this phenomenon. Advertisers work very hard to help our minds relate their products to associations we find pleasing. They do this with subtle cues and frequent repetition.

There are few middle-aged people who could not complete the following sentences:

> "Winston tastes good like. . ."
> "Ivory is _____ percent pure."
> "Pepsi Cola hits _____."
> "Plop plop, fizz fizz _____."

Even though these slogans have been off the air for decades, we've heard them and thousands of other advertising messages so often that it's hard to forget them. These messages have been programmed into us when we hear them, read them, and even when they are played as background radio sound in our homes.

We do "hear" and process information that comes to us below the threshold of consciousness. For many people, the chief roadblock to success or bouncing back from a slump is the subliminal messages with which their minds work.

Denis Waitley tells of a woman who was brought completely sedated into a hospital operating room. Several of the medical staff made derogatory remarks and joked about the "great white whale" as they performed the surgery.

The surgery went well, but the woman seemed to be having a slower than normal recovery. When a nurse talked with the patient, the woman confided that she was very emotionally upset by the procedure. She felt an inexplicable distrust and hostility toward the doctors who had performed the operation. She couldn't quite pinpoint the source of her feelings, but she sensed that the surgery had been a humiliating experience.

How could this woman, who was completely anesthetized, know that her doctors had been flippant and insulting? Their insults had registered on her subconscious.

Perhaps the most famous account of subliminal programming is an experiment in a movie theater in the 1950's. During the showing of the movie, the messages "eat popcorn" and "drink Coke" were flashed on the screen repeatedly, each at a tiny fraction of a second. The message could not be seen or "read" by the conscious mind, but the subconscious apparently picked it up, resulting in sharp increases in popcorn and Coke sales at the concessions stand.

As the potential of subliminal programming becomes more widely known, a number of ethical issues arise. If we can't consciously hear the message, how do we know what is being said? Could alien beings program us "wrong"? Not likely. As with self-hypnosis, our mind weighs incoming messages against our basic value system and will likely tune out messages that contradict our most deep-seated beliefs.

We script our life around the clock. When messages are played over and over, they get results. Self-talk is the way we take control of our feelings and senses. Subliminal tapes can help program our mind for success, breaking through old "scripting" and motivating us to new levels of achievement.

But how do we determine which of the available tapes work best? I recommend that you first consider the credibility of the authors. Try tapes from people whose professional reputation is on the line. Buy from reputable publishers. Try subliminal tapes of music or neutral sounds like ocean waves.[1] Play them regularly, even while you are doing other things. That's the beauty of subliminal tapes, they work on your subconscious when your conscious mind is busy with something else.

Specific Behaviors that Tap Your Mental Powers
(☑ Check off when you've tried them)

☐ 1. Using the techniques described in this chapter, tap the power of imaging. Set specific times for imaging each day for at least 21 days. Set objectives for what you want to accomplish. Jot down in your daily planner the feelings, reactions, and ideas that come to you when imaging.

☐ 2. Create your mental "hideaway." Visualize and constantly sharpen the picture of this special, peaceful place. Use all your senses. Then practice going to your imaged hideaway as you relax and move into self-hypnosis.

☐ 3. Assemble your personal "board of directors." Whom do you know that would be excellent role models for you? How can you get to know them better, so that you can model their specific actions and thought patterns? Write out the names of these people and describe their attributes that you would like to achieve.

☐ 4. Try a modeling project. Select one person you know whose behavior you would like to model. For example, if someone you know is good at woodworking and you'd like to do woodworking, make arrangements to visit with that person and learn his techniques. If a friend of yours is a good Italian cook, watch over his shoulder and model his expertise. If another friend is exceptionally well organized, see if she'll let you observe and model what she does. (Most people are flattered when you say you'd like to learn what they know.)

☐ 5. Purchase some reputable subliminal tapes and listen to them at least six times. Better yet, play subliminal tapes as a background while you go about your daily activities. Use a headset or other tape player, preferably with auto-reverse.

[1] A set of tapes I have been very happy with is Denis Waitley and Thomas Budzynski's *The Subliminal Winner,* produced by Nightingale-Conant Corporation.

CHAPTER 6

BACK TO BASIC TIME AND TASK MANAGEMENT _____

> *He who chases two rabbits goes hungry to bed.*
> —Indian saying

> *This guy was such a time manager he missed the slot in a revolving door and it threw him off for a week!*
> —Author

A farmer well-known for raising prize-winning hogs was visited by a journalist from the *Farmer's Gazette.* "How do you consistently raise such fine hogs?" the writer asked.

"Beats me," replied the farmer. "But you're welcome to follow me around for a while and see what I do."

The farmer then went down to the orchard where his hogs were rooting. One by one and with considerable effort, he lifted each pig up in his arms until the hog could eat apples from one of the trees.

"That sure takes a lot of time," commented the journalist.

"Sure," replied the farmer philosophically, "but what's time to a pig?"

The more important question for us is, what's time to a success-seeking human?

Time is the stuff of life. It's our most precious resource. And if you're experiencing a slump in your career, it may be because you've let too much of this valuable stuff slip away. To "Do Things Right" we make mental efforts (as described in the last chapter), but we also need to be sure that we strive for greater efficiency and effectiveness in time management.

Think about your time this way: We all have 86,400 seconds to work with each day. Pretend that each second is a penny. You'd start each day with $840 in your account at the First National Bank of Time. Every day, another $840 is deposited for you. The only stipulation is that you must spend it all. At the end of the day, any remaining balance will be swept away, gone forever.

How will you spend your $840? Some will be spent on maintenance (sleeping, eating, exercise) but, we hope, some will also be invested in activities that pay big dividends in the future. Benefits like goal achievement and value congruence can be achieved on time, if we use time effectively. Management guru Peter Drucker says that "Time is our most precious resource. If we can't manage time, we will not be able to manage anything else."

Time and Task Management Tools

The best tool for developing the action patterns that make the most of your time is a planner system. Bookstores and office supply houses are well stocked with a wide variety of planners, to-do list forms, and calendars. You've probably already used several of these over the years. While formats differ, the purpose is the same: to help you get organized and better spend your daily 86,400 seconds.

A planner needn't be elaborate or expensive. Some people succumb to the status symbolism of certain planners. A trendy $150 organizer includes a map of the London subway system, but if you want a snakeskin cover, it costs $550! Such a deal.

Snakeskin covers are irrelevant, but planners do work—at least if used correctly. An appropriately designed planner can tremendously boost your power to be productive.

If you've used planners and they didn't seem to help all that much, maybe you've been using the wrong tool. Here's what to look for in a good planner (with or without snakeskin):

Characteristics of the Best Planners

A planner needs five things to make it work for you:

1. A place to list and assign priorities to tasks. (I'll show you how to develop a priority task list in just a moment.)
2. A place to record notes and follow-up information.
3. A place for goals and values. Having these incorporated into your planning tool is a powerful way to make sure they are realized.
4. A place for frequently referred-to information, especially addresses, phone numbers, perhaps birthdays, etc.
5. Flexibility to meet your needs.

Overcoming Resistance to Planning

Some people resist planning. Some say they don't like to feel bound by a plan—they want to stay "flexible." Others claim to do all their planning in their heads. And more than a few simply don't see the value to planning. They live by wandering around.

I'm going to try to help you see the value of planning, because if you value something, you'll do it.

A *Business Update* report states: "As a general rule, spending only 5 percent of the day planning can help managers achieve 95 percent of their goals." It continues: "Planning prevents managers from doing the wrong things the wrong way at the wrong time, and it forces them to answer the question, 'What really needs to be accomplished?' "

Planning is a good idea because, according to *Business Update,* "It's always best to perform activities sequentially rather than simultaneously. In fact, we *can't* do things simultaneously and do them well. The idea behind time management is determining *how to do things sequentially."*

The Nuts and Bolts of Time and Task Management

I recommend that you devote a minimum of 10-15 minutes a day solely to planning. Use a planner system you like.[1] Then apply the steps described below, and you will see a significant increase in your personal effectiveness. First-time users of a planner report immediate productivity increases of 25 percent or more!

Step 1. **Develop a priority task list for each day.**

Prioritizing tasks helps us sort them out, determine which need to be attacked first and which can be saved for later.

Here's how: List the specific tasks you want or need to spend your time on for a particular day. Using your own "shorthand," list the items you wish to accomplish. It might read something like this: complete the XYZ report, get stamps, attend Billy's softball game, eat more fish, keep date with husband or child.

---

[1] The Plan-It Life Organizer is shown in the illustration. See the back of the book for ordering information.

At this stage, don't be overly concerned with the *importance* of the items; just get in the habit of listing *all* nonroutine tasks that you want to accomplish that day. Don't bother listing all those tasks you do automatically (e.g., brushing teeth, doing the dishes, waiting on customers.)

TRY THIS:

Balance Your Planning among the Three Life Dimensions

To maintain a sense of balance in your planning, check yourself to see if you are targeting activities from the three areas likely to bring you the most satisfaction:

> **career,**
> **relationships,**
> **self.**

On the sample sheet from the Plan-It Life Organizer, the task list section is shaded to remind you to set priorities in the three areas. Remember that each of the three areas is important in your life.

A "structured system" (such as your career task list) will always be more compelling than an "unstructured system" (your good intentions about relationships or self-improvement). Maintain balance—if all your tasks are from one category, you'll experience an imbalance that will distort your life.

Step 2. **Assign a letter priority to each item on your list.**

Use *A,B,C,* or * (star) and place the letter *A* next to items that *must* be done. These are critical to you, though you alone determine whether they are critical or not based on your values and goals. Tasks required either by outside forces (e.g., your boss) or internal ones (e.g., a strong personal commitment) will normally receive an *A* priority. Be careful not to assign *A*'s to *every* task. Giving everything an *A* defeats the purpose of prioritizing.

Use the letter *B* to indicate *should do* items. These tasks aren't quite as critical as the A tasks, yet it is worth spending time to achieve them.

The letter *C* is for *could do* items. These tasks are worth listing and thinking about—and, if you complete your *A*'s and *B*'s, worth doing.

A * indicates an item that is *urgent*—something that *must* be done and done *now*. It is both important and vital and must be done right away. Occasionally such a job occurs during a work day (i.e, a crisis). When you add starred items to your list, drop whatever else you're doing, even an *A* item and complete the starred tasks first.

Use a star very sparingly. Normally, urgent tasks are not factored into your dedicated planning time. They pop up and scream "do me now!" Be careful, however, to determine that an item really *is* important before you bump the rest of your plan to squeeze it in. Just because something makes a lot of noise doesn't necessarily mean that it must be done instantly. Don't let a false urgency override an important task you've planned.

Step 3. **Assign a number to your task.**

Your plan of attack can be further sharpened by assigning a number to each task. Some people, however, see little value in numbering tasks once the priority letter has been assigned. You can decide what works best for you in this matter.

The best use of the numbering system is as a chronological indicator. Ask, "Which task should I do first?" If you have a meeting at two in the afternoon and it's an *A* item, the meeting may not be *A-1* simply because other priorities must be attended to earlier in the day.

Step 4. **Use completion symbols: the payoff.**

After you complete the tasks listed in your planner, you deserve a reward. This reward takes the form of a completion symbol.

Here are several completion symbols, starting with one that feels the best to me:

> (✓) The check mark symbol indicates that a task has been completed. That should feel good. Many people prefer to make their check marks in red as a reminder of how productive they have been.

(→) A second symbol, an arrow, is used when a task needs to be rescheduled. Perhaps a meeting has been cancelled or an appointment changed, or the task simply could not be completed because you were wrapped up in another matter.

IMPORTANT: Whenever you use the arrow, be sure to reschedule the task to another day in the planner. Using the arrow and rescheduling the task for another day earns you the right to forget that task for awhile. You'll be reminded of it automatically on the new day you scheduled. And it'll be there when you do your daily personal planning.

(O) A third symbol often used is a circle placed in the margin to the left of the completion symbol column to indicate that the task has been delegated to someone else.

It may be that you've asked your spouse to pick up a book of stamps on the way home from work or assigned a child to clean out the garage. Or, it may be a more formal kind of delegation, in which you've asked a colleague or subordinate to complete a task. If several people are reporting to you, you may want to use the circle centered with the initial of the person to whom the task has been delegated. When the task has been completed, you should then place a check mark in the "completed" column.

(X) A fourth symbol is an "X," to indicate that a task has been deleted. It may mean that you blew it and it just didn't get done, or it may mean that you've reconsidered and determined that this task simply isn't worth doing. Remember, you are in charge. If you schedule a task but later decide it really isn't what you want to do—so be it. You X it out.

		Priority tasks	Schedule	Notes
		Thursday		
✓	A¹	Complete XYZ report		
→	C²	Get Stamps		
X	B³	Call Bill re: wigits	8	
✓	B⁴	Jog 5+ miles	9	Staff mtg.
✓	A²	Get data for budget	10	
X	C²	✓ with Harry re: golf	11	↓
✓	B¹	Call Paula re: article	12	
(H)	B²	Deposit check	1	
✓	B⁵	Catch up on mail	2	
→	A³	Talk to Ray about billing	3	Call Bill re: wigits
			4	
			5	
✓	A⁴	Billy's ballgame	6³⁰ Billy's game	
X	C¹	Read Lisa a story		

		Priority tasks	Schedule
		Friday	
		Mtg. w/ Carol	
		Date with Helen	
		Get Stamps	8
		Talk to Ray about billing	

Assume that tomorrow is Monday. Complete the three steps, and begin listing and prioritizing what you need to do "tomorrow." Include both business and personal tasks—especially those congruent with your core values. Write your plan on the form shown on the following page.

plan·it **life organizer**	Week of 19	This week		
A Must do ✓ Completed B Should do → Moved C Could do ( ) Delegated ★ Urgent—DO NOW ✗ Deleted				

Monday

		Priority tasks	Schedule	Notes
			8	
			9	
			10	
			11	
			12	
			1	
			2	
			3	
			4	
			5	
				✓ Journal ⬜

Tuesday

		Priority tasks	Schedule	Notes
			8	
			9	
			10	
			11	
			12	
			1	
			2	
			3	
			4	
			5	
				✓ Journal ⬜

Wednesday

		Priority tasks	Schedule	Notes
			8	
			9	
			10	
			11	
			12	
			1	
			2	
			3	
			4	
			5	
				✓ Journal ⬜

Incorporating Goals and Values in Your Daily Planning

Your priority task list should provide an overview of your daily activities. But how do these activities tie in with your long-term values and goals?

For most people, they don't. And that's why people often fail to achieve what's really important to them. The challenge is to

make your daily activities consistent with your goals and values.

The best planner system is more than just a calendar. It should have a place to record your core values, value-aligning activities, and short-term goals. The Plan-It Life Organizer does just that. But if the planner you use doesn't, try to modify it.

While planning your daily priority tasks, make sure that the goals and values you previously articulated for yourself are evident. The "life plan" section of a planner is where you *record your core values and value-aligning activities.* It is very important to refer to them. The more often these are reviewed, the more likely they will become a part of your being. Your daily plan should reflect "the big picture" described in your life plan.

Likewise, your yearly plan and monthly plans should promote specific *tasks* relevant to your daily *activities.* For example, if your life plan indicates a high value for "health and vigor," your value-aligning activities might well include regular exercise programs of walking or aerobics. For your yearly plan record, a priority task might be to power walk 500 miles or participate in an aerobics class at least three times each week for the calendar year.

You then translate your annual goal into walking 40 miles or attending 12 aerobic sessions each month. This goal should be entered on your monthly plan page. Since you have decided that you want to walk or exercise a specific amount during a month, it is simple to break down the monthly goal into daily objectives. Your priority tasks for a particular day may be to run three miles or attend an exercise class. When you write that down, you have translated your values and long-term goals into daily tasks, and as you perform your tasks, you will be focusing your energy in ways that relate to your life goals.

TRY THIS: **Translating Values into Activities**

Take a moment to translate one of your core values into a daily activity. Envision your core value at the base of a pyramid. The value-aligning activities occupy the middle of the pyramid. At the top of the pyramid go the daily activities that will move you, even if only slightly, in the direction of achievement and value congruence.

Daily Actions

Monthly and Weekly Activities

Long- and Short-term Goals

Values

Accomplishments Do Not Always Bring Satisfaction

One criticism of planner systems in general is that they push people to list and check off tasks without regard for whether those tasks have any value. By having daily tasks reflect our goals and core values, we minimize the problem of galloping off in the wrong direction. But one more benefit arises from value-based planning: We get more satisfaction in life.

People who use simple "to-do" lists or planners that don't link their actions with their values run the risk of suffering "to-do list frustration." This occurs when we keep adding to our task list, making our expectations of what can be done fly off into infinity.

We can never experience satisfaction if we keep increasing our expectations. One way to look at this is through the simple mathematical formula:

$$S = A/E$$

Satisfaction equals Accomplishment divided by Expectations. If we keep pushing ourselves to increase our expectations of what we can do—keep pushing ourselves to do more and do better, regardless of how well we are already progressing—we will never experience satisfaction. A feeling of constantly falling short, instead, causes us increased stress and frustration.

Keep expectations realistic. Avoid the tendency to add to your task list beyond what is reasonable and you will greatly enhance your sense of satisfaction with what you accomplish.

Recording Key Data in Your Planner

The typical executive spends 90 minutes a day retrieving information he or she needs, according to one study. Each of us inevitably needs some bit of information that seems to have fallen between the cracks.

To reduce retrieval time, get into the habit of jotting down notes and commitments *in a standardized place.* Here, too, an effective planner system can be of enormous help, if it has a place to record notes.

Here's an example. Suppose you talk to a salesperson about purchasing a new car. You are told that you can buy the car for $14,500, with a financing charge of 10.5% interest between now and July 1. Also, the salesperson tells you that you can finance for up to four years at that rate and he'll throw in an extended warranty package. You need to let him know by next Friday if you want the car.

Being the effective time and task manager that you are, you have written all this critical data in your planner. On Thursday evening you visit the dealership only to discover that the sales rep you talked with quit yesterday. A new sales person offers you an entirely different and less advantageous deal. What do you do? You pull out your secret weapon: the planner where you recorded the terms previously quoted. If the dealership honors the deal you've recorded—and I'll bet it will—you've paid for the cost of your planner many times over.

It makes sense to jot down information regularly. For example, record the phone numbers of people you talk to, in case you need to call them again. Note when you mailed something to someone, in case it doesn't arrive and you need to know when it was sent. Price quotes, commitments exchanged, reminders about someone's family, or an interesting idea—all can be captured quickly if we take just a moment to record them in the planner.

Locating these bits of information is easy if your planner has a week-at-a-glance format. It takes only moments to review as much as a full year of pages.

I had an experience that brought home to me the value of this process. I recalled that several years ago, sometime in the winter, I had received a price quote on some materials I needed for my business. They were items I buy only occasionally, and I couldn't remember the figures or even the name of the company.

Because I had jotted down the data in my Plan-It Life Organizer and I had stored back pages from that planner in a loose-leaf binder, I was able to locate that information in a matter of minutes. I simply reviewed the winter months—I remembered that the ground was covered with snow—and found the vendor's name, address, phone number, and price quote. This saved me hours of research. And using a planner to record information can work for you in hundreds of unanticipated ways.

One final note: Use your planner for this recording process. If you rely on pink note slips, scraps of paper, or the backs of envelopes, you will inevitably lose the one bit of information you need most. These "butterflies," as one time management consultant calls them, too often fly and leave you frustrated.

Specific Behaviors that Build the Planning Habit
(☑ Check off when you've tried them)

☐ 1. Daily planning activates the achievement process. Commit today to use a planner system—one that meets the criteria for usefulness described in this chapter. Doing so translates your visions and goals into daily rituals.

☐ 2. Set aside 10–15 minutes each day for writing in your planner. For many people, the first thing in the morning is a good time. Others prefer the last moments each evening, so the unconscious mind can work on the tasks while they sleep. Either time is fine. Just be sure to do it. Initially, you may want to write "planning" on your priority task list, so that you can have the satisfaction of checking it off!

☐ 3. Remember that a planner shouldn't create stress for you. It's your tool, not your master. Keep your system flexible and personal. Use as much or as little of the system as is comfortable for you. And remember: A = S/E. Don't overload your expectations until you cannot take satisfaction from the progress you are making.

The difference between successful people and unsuccessful people lies in the habits they have developed, good or bad. Start the habit of daily planning today—and stick with it. In doing so, you tap into the power source of constructive action patterns. You do things right.

BEST IDEA 4

Treat People Well
The Golden Rule for Interpersonal Relations

CHAPTER 7

COMMUNICATE THE "WIN-WIN" IDEA _____

> *The most important thing I learned in school was how to communicate.*
>
> —Lee Iacocca

> *There are very few people who don't become more interesting when they stop talking.*
>
> —Author

People who bounce back from slumps and setbacks inevitably do so with a little help from their friends. In times of personal change, we need to mobilize our support network. Leaders—and survivors—are not people who go it alone in this complex world. They are the people who inspire others to accomplish things together and, in so doing, they too are rewarded.

We need to communicate with people for two reasons: (1) to gather needed information, and (2) to elicit emotional support.

We all are involved in a web of relationships: family, co-workers, associates, friends, and professional contacts. People who draw strength from these relationships are able to tackle challenges that they couldn't tackle alone. Problems do not seem as overwhelming when shared with others who care. Through such sharing you gain energy, resources, and strength.[1]

Communication is the means for creating and cementing relationships. As we communicate effectively, we build rapport and support. This chapter discusses three types of communication that can produce "win-win" relationships with others:

- *Intrapersonal (or internal) communication*
- *Interpersonal communication,* and
- *Networking communication.*

_____

[1] For an excellent self-help workbook on this topic, order *Managing Personal Change,* using the order form in the back of this book.

IntraPersonal Communication: The Voice Within

We've already discussed self-talk. In Chapter 1, we saw how what we say to ourselves affects our self-concept and in Chapter 5, how to tap our mental powers via internal conversations and imaging. There is a clear relationship between the messages we process in our mind and the world we create for ourself. Our relationships with others depend largely on how we see the world.

Effective self-talk helps us be authentic—true to our true selves. Effective self-talk promotes helping us know who we are. It may seem inauthentic to act as if you are already what you seek to be, but it isn't. Authenticity, or the quality of being realistically aware of where you are in your journey through life, involves self-acceptance. People who are authentic do not play false roles prescribed by other people.

It is helpful to act as if we have advanced along our personal timeline and are *now* a new and improved version of our present self.

I recognize four phases in our quest for authenticity. We start the cyclical process by recognizing who we *really* are. In this first phase, which I call the IDENTITY phase, we clarify our self-concept, recognizing our strengths and shortcomings. We unconditionally accept ourselves despite any past mistakes or losses.

Next, we determine a course of action. We set goals and targets and establish a plan of action. Then we DO what we've set out to do. With persistence and effort, we then progress into the ACHIEVE phase. Now, having had new and successful experiences, we find ourselves at a new starting point: the NEW ME

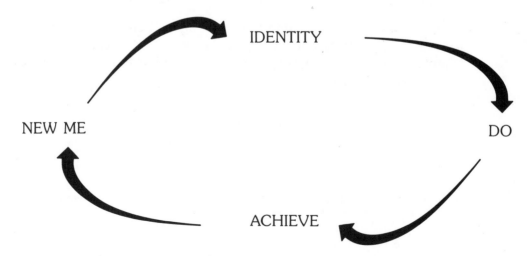

IDENTITY

NEW ME   DO

ACHIEVE

The cycle then repeats itself, propelling us to new plateaus. Underlying the process is our sense of authenticity—seeing ourself and others realistically. Remember, others have their own cycles and they may differ from where you are right now. That is only natural and perfectly acceptable. We have no right to demand that others be different from what they are.

Vital to authenticity is admitting mistakes—not groveling in self-pity, remorse, or self-condemnation, but taking a realistic look at where we are now and how we got there.

In the novel *Lonesome Dove,* by Larry McMurtry, a great piece of dialogue occurs between the two lead cowboy characters, Gus McRae and Woodrow Call. Call, the stereotypical "strong, silent type," is a stoic leader but almost totally lacking in expressiveness, utterly incapable of voicing his emotions. McRae is his opposite, a frontier philosopher who likes nothing better than to "jaw" about almost anything. The difference between the two men leads to this conversation:

> Gus: "You're so sure you're right it doesn't matter to you whether people talk to you or not. I'm glad I've been wrong enough to keep in practice."
>
> "Why would you want to keep in practice being wrong?" Call asked. "I'd think it would be something you'd try to avoid."
>
> "You can't avoid it, you've got to learn to handle it," Gus said. "If you only come face to face with your own mistakes once or twice in your life it's bound to be painful. I face mine every day—that way they ain't usually much worse than a dry shave."[2]

Past mistakes, real or imagined, are beyond our control. All people make mistakes, but while recognizing them is imperative, dwelling on them is counterproductive.

Styles of Distorted Thinking

The internal conversations that so powerfully shape our sense of self also color the way we see the world around us, including other people. To build "win-win" relationships with others requires a realistic perspective of the way things are.

[2] Larry McMurtry, *Lonesome Dove,* p. 625.

TRY THIS: Ridding Yourself of Distorted Thinking

Following each of the descriptions of distorted thinking below, write a brief example you've experienced. These examples may be thoughts you have had or ones you've seen in others. If you recognize that you distort thoughts, set an action target to change your thought patterns.

1. *Polarized Thinking*

    As we discussed in Chapter 1, simplistic, either/or, black/white, or good/bad thinking overlooks the vast middle ground between the extremes. Such polarized thinking leads people to believe that they must either be perfect or are failures. Polarized thinkers frequently use lots of -*est* words, superlatives such as big*gest*, b*est*, bright*est*, ugl*iest*, etc. In reality, few things fit into such extreme categories. (Review pages 33-36 if this continues to be a problem area for you.)

    Your examples of polarized thinking:

2. *Overgeneralization*

    It is a mistake to come to a general conclusion based on a single incident or piece of evidence. If something bad happened once, victims of overgeneralization expect it to happen over and over. If they were terminated from a job, they think it'll happen again.

    Such faulty reasoning can lead to self-fulfilling expectations. If we expect something unpleasant to happen or someone to do something stupid, the chances increase that it will indeed happen. If it doesn't happen, we might *even imagine* that it's happened just to prove ourselves right.

    List your examples of overgeneralization:

3. *Personalization*

People prone to personalization think that everything people do or say is some kind of a reaction to them. They take things personally even when they are not intended to be so. They also compare themselves to others, trying to determine who's smarter, better looking, etc. People who fall into this trap fail to remember that we are all unique. It's not necessary to compare yourself to others, nor is it important what others think about you. The important thing is how you feel about yourself.

Your examples of personalization:

4. *Fallacy of Change*

Some people expect that other people will change to suit them if they just pressure or cajole them enough. They feel a need to change people, because their hopes for happiness depend so much on them. In reality, we can seldom change others—they live in the realm of the uncontrollable. Our happiness, however, need not depend on the approval of others.

Your examples of the fallacy of change thinking:

5. *Need to Be Right*

People who need to "be right" are continually on trial to prove that their opinions and actions are correct. Being wrong is unthinkable and they will go to any lengths to demonstrate their infallibility. Likewise, they cannot tolerate the opinions of others, who are so obviously wrong. They'll argue to the death for what is right. In reality, of course, we are all wrong sometimes, even when it comes to heartfelt convictions. No one is right 100 percent of the time.

Your examples of the need to be right:

6. *Filtering Out the Positive*
   To take negative details and magnify them while filtering out positive aspects of a situation is to court misery. If a person pays you three compliments and one criticism, some people dwell on the criticism and tune out the compliments. Likewise, once they have formed an opinion about a person or situation, they filter out any ideas that may contradict their opinion. They perceive others as they expect them to be—and miss out on who they really are.

   Your examples of filtering out the positive:

7. *Shoulds and Oughts*
   Some people have a list of ironclad rules about how they and others should act. They feel angry when others break the rules and guilty if they violate any rules.

   Your examples of shoulds and oughts:

Internal communication patterns affect how we react to others and they to us. Understanding how we think and the fallacies to which we are prone help us form stronger relationships with others.

Interpersonal Communication

Communicating with others allows us to create a support network that will sustain us in times of need. How can we build the best possible network? Here are a few ideas:

Improve Listening Skills

The greatest single tool for effective communication with other people is *listening.* There is no such thing as an unpopular listener. Unfortunately, good listeners are scarce. For most people, listening means impatiently waiting for a place to insert, "That reminds me. . ."

To build and sustain a support network, we need to develop good listening skills. Since so few people know how to listen, being a good listener is an excellent way to distinguish yourself.[3] Studies show that only about 25 percent of people rate themselves as good listeners. Far too many of us think of listening as something passive—something we *sit back and do* while we are waiting for our turn to talk.

In reality, listening requires *active* mental effort. Ironically, unlike speaking, writing, and reading, listening is a communication skill seldom taught in school. People who do learn to listen well not only learn a lot but become very popular.

There are two general types of listening:

supportive listening, and
retention listening.

Supportive listening is used when our primary purpose is to convey our support for the speaker. For example, if a person is telling you about an unfortunate incident and there is nothing you can do about it, use support listening to extend a sense of sympathy. Let yours be the shoulder the speaker can lean on.

Retention listening is used when our primary purpose is to process and retain information presented orally. For example, if someone is giving you directions or instructions, you should use retention listening techniques.

These tips will help you improve your listening skills:

1. *Look at those* to whom you are listening. Give them your undivided attention. If you can't give them your attention, say so and arrange another time when you can. By looking at a speaker, we pick up many subtle, nonverbal cues that help us understand the message and accurately receive the communication.

---

[3] For an excellent, hands-on workbook on improving listening skills, order *The Business of Listening,* using the form in the back of this book.

2. *Work at it.* Become an *active* listener, deeply involved in what is said. Don't let your mind drift off or mentally rehearse what you'll say next.

3. *Use supportive and clarifying comments.* One approach is called the "uh huh" response. As a person talks to you, periodically say "uh huh" or a similar phrase to let him know that you are "with him." Incidently, this is particularly important when using the telephone, which does not permit the communication of nonverbal messages. If you are silent, the speaker may wonder if you are still there.

You also convey supportiveness by simply repeating the speaker's words. This permits you to express your support while clarifying the speaker's meaning. For example, Betty and Linda are talking:

Betty: I got so mad at that stupid computer I wanted to throw it across the room.

Linda: You got mad at the computer?

Betty: You bet I did. I have never seen such a piece of junk.

Linda: A piece of junk, huh?

Betty: I've got to talk to Harry about a new machine.

Linda: Good idea.

4. Use *open-ended questions* to clarify the speaker's points. An open-ended question is simply one that cannot be answered "yes" or "no" or with a one-word answer. For example, Henry and Tony pose open-ended questions:

Bob: If I have to watch one more sloppy sales presentation, I think I'll go nuts.

Henry: What bothers you the most about the presentations, Bob?

Tom: I really don't think you've treated me fairly, Tony. You seem to give everyone else more opportunities, while I'm still stuck in the same old job.

Tony: I'd like to understand what you're saying. In what ways do you think I've given other people more opportunities?

5. *Use thoughtful pauses.* When people ask your opinion, it is often wise to pause for a moment before responding. This suggests to them that you are thoughtful and that their question is worth pondering. And taking time to think before you speak may enable you to offer a helpful and wise response.

6. *Imagine that you'll be asked to report what you hear.* If we approach listening with the notion that we will be required to communicate what we hear to others, we will listen more carefully. This is especially important in retention listening.

7. *Repeat key ideas back to the speaker for clarification.* This has several benefits. It lets the speaker know that you are following the thoughts and that you consider it important to understand what he or she is saying. If you do not understand something, ask the speaker to clarify it. Don't pretend to understand when you really don't: better to admit lack of understanding and receive clarification than to be left in the dark.

Feedback

One of the most critical ingredients in bouncing back from setbacks is to be *receptive* to feedback—even that from your most severe critics. This, of course, can be painful. But it can also be *exceptionally* valuable.

TRY THIS: **Feedback Receptiveness Quiz**

Answer the following questions honestly. Do not share your answers. As a general rule:

	Yes	No	
1.	☐	☐	I get embarrassed when people point out my mistakes.
2.	☐	☐	I resent people telling me what they think of my shortcomings.
3.	☐	☐	I regularly ask friends and associates I trust to comment on how I'm doing.
4.	☐	☐	I know how to offer constructive criticism to others in a sensitive way.
5.	☐	☐	I like people who tell me their reactions to my activities, because it will help me adapt my future behavior.

If you answered "yes" to items 1 and 2, you may be putting up some resistance that could deter you from obtaining useful feedback. We are normally uncomfortable when we receive harsh or insensitive feedback, but even that can be valuable if we take it in perspective. Even our worst critic can provide a "gift" of good advice if we don't allow emotion to blind us. Successful people learn how to look for good advice even when it's buried under a lot of worthless noise.

If you answered "yes" to items 3 and 4, you are creating a climate where helpful feedback is accepted and expected. Organizations fostering such a climate are typically positive places to work and successful in achieving their goals. In a similar fashion, receptive individuals can benefit from others' advice.

If you answered "yes" to item 5, you are probably a little unusual. But you're on the right track.

We never really do know how we are coming across to others unless we seek *feedback*. Feedback is a critical ingredient to bouncing back.

An unhappy customer can be a business' best friend. Feedback is critical to an effective business. One study indicated that, on average, dissatisfied customers tell 10 other people about their dissatisfaction; about 20 percent tell 20 or more people. It costs five times more to gain a new customer than to keep an existing one. A business cannot afford to lose its current customers.

A most interesting fact is that even the most dissatisfied customers stick with a business if they receive an indication that their complaint has been heard and acted upon. The most dangerous situation is when unhappy customers do *not* tell the company of their dissatisfaction. In a sense, an unhappy customer is a company's best friend, *providing the company gets feedback.* Therefore, enlightened companies go to great lengths to make it easy for customers to comment about service.

This same principle can apply to our daily interactions with friends, associates, and business contacts.

Feedback receptiveness is an attitude. Less successful companies and people prefer to be ostriches. They bury their heads and tune out all negative comments. In so doing, they never learn what they need to know. Confirming and clarifying how we are relating to others requires feedback. Feedback becomes the control system for self-management.

Complete the following sentence in your own words:

> I plan to encourage useful feedback by. . .

For most people, giving criticism (even in a constructive way) is risky business. When people first offer criticism, they watch very closely to gauge others' response. The reaction they receive will usually determine whether they will offer feedback again. This means that *you* have an opportunity to avoid turning off future feedback that could be valuable to you. Tips for encouraging feedback:

1. **Don't be defensive. Listen—don't explain or justify.** Learn to bite your tongue. While someone criticizes you is not the time to explain or justify your action, even if you feel the criticism is unwarranted or stems from a misunderstanding. When you request feedback, the burden is on you to listen and try to understand. This does not mean you are obligated to believe or accept the information, but it does allow you to try to understand why others feel and react as they do. Defensiveness stifles feedback. It tells others you are more interested in justifying yourself than in understanding what is being said.

2. **Ask for more information, especially for specifics.** When you are engaged in a feedback session, there is an opportunity to obtain additional information. Honest questions will support and encourage a continual flow of feedback. For example, say, "That's extremely helpful. Tell me more. Is there anything else I should know about that?"

3. **Express an honest reaction.** The person giving the feedback wants to know your reaction to the information being presented. The best guideline is to express your honest reaction. "I'm a little surprised you said that, but you probably have a point." or "I'm not sure what to say. I never even thought of that, but I will from now on."

4. Thank those providing feedback and plan for the future. Let people know that you realize how risky giving feedback can be and express your appreciation for their efforts. This might also be a good time to plan for future feedback sessions. These should be less disturbing and more productive than the first one, because you have demonstrated your receptiveness. Most leaders make the receipt of feedback a regular and continuing process.

You should realize that few people can handle the four points presented above. Not because they wouldn't benefit from it, but because they are afraid to hear it. *It takes courage to hear and request criticism!*

The successful person is willing to do what the unsuccessful person is not. Getting feedback to provide direction and control is a classic example of such an action. When you learn to benefit from feedback, you'll reap a rich reward.

Feedback Checklist

Think back to the last time you received criticism from someone else. Did you:

Yes	No	
☐	☐	Avoid defending or explaining yourself until the full criticism was expressed?
☐	☐	Understand the speaker's point of view as best you could?
☐	☐	Ask for elaboration or clarification?
☐	☐	Express an honest reaction?
☐	☐	Thank the person for the feedback?

Is your future behavior regarding feedback likely to change?

Yes ☐   No ☐

Timing

Just a quick thought about timing of messages:

> *Nothing impresses so significantly as immediate follow-through.*

Fast follow-through is a simple idea but a good one. To build stronger "win-win" relationships, do what you say you'll do and do it immediately.

Timing is an often overlooked aspect of effective communication. A thank-you note received months late lacks sincerity. A promised deed done only after being reminded several times is less valued than a spontaneous and immediate action.

Use your planner system to make sure that commitments made are honored. Build a reputation for always doing what you say you'll do—and doing it immediately.

Enthusiasm

Interpersonal relationships are strengthened by shared enthusiasm. The old cliché that enthusiasm is contagious is true. How do we convey enthusiasm to others? Mainly through voice and body movement. The messages communicated by our voice and body tend to be trusted, because it is virtually impossible to contradict true intent with nonverbal communication. And nonverbal conveys as much as 77 percent of the message.

Don't hold back on expressing enthusiasm just because you are in a structured environment. For example, don't assume that a presentation in a meeting needs to be bereft of enthusiasm just because the occasion is somewhat formal.

Say what you feel. Can you imagine returning to college after a fabulous Christmas vacation and saying to your roommates, "I have several experiences I'd like to share with you." You'd sound a little more excited than that! Expressing what you feel is an important aspect of being authentic.

Building Rapport

Experts in neurolinguistic programming believe that we can build rapport with others instantly if we respond to them in the same "voice" they use when talking to us. If a person's speech is direct, emphatic, and loud, we can build rapport with him by using a similar intonation and volume. If a person speaks slowly and quietly, responding in kind creates rapport.

TRY THIS: **Building Rapport Instantly**

Listen carefully to people who talk with you. Then try to mimic their tone and volume as you respond to them. Use some of the same terms they use. Observe the effect of their vocal imitation.

Networking Communication

A network of friends and close associates is a tremendously valuable asset. Go out of your way to make *and keep* friends. A key to maintaining friendship is maintaining close contact. Remember your friends' interests. Then take *every* opportunity to:

- mail them a news clipping about something that interests them
- call them with useful information
- buy some small item you know they'd like
- take time to seek their opinion on a sporting event or news story in which you know they have an interest.

Do so without expectation of anything in return. But the law of reciprocity—the social "law" that makes people seek to return kindness for kindness—will take effect. When you are thoughtful toward others, they will be thoughtful toward you.

TRY THIS: Networking

List five people who are important members of your network,
people you could count on in need and who can count on you,
too. Beside their name, describe two or three of their interests.
Finally, set a goal to send something or convey some message to
each of them within the next month. If you can't find a relevant
clipping, small gift, or reason for a call, plan to write a general note
of thanks—thanks for being your friend or thanks for being helpful.
Such notes can greatly strengthen relationships.

	Network	Interests	Goal
1.			
2.			
3.			
4.			
5.			

(Don't forget to add these goals in your planner.)

Create Your Personal Board of Directors

One of the most powerful ideas for bouncing back is to create "You,
Inc." Doing so simply requires shifting your point of view and comparing
yourself to a corporation.

As a corporation, you exist to provide goods and services of various
types to your customers. As CEO in your corporation, you constantly
make important decisions.

Corporations often seek outside points of view to gauge if they are on
track. This overview is provided by its board of directors. Members of
the board offer objective advice to the corporation's leader: yourself.

Each of us can create a board of directors by mentally assembling
people whose opinions we trust. These people are our "opinion
leaders." Naturally, we value the opinions of some people in some

matters but not in others. None of us possesses universal expertise. For example, while we may trust our mother's advice about relationships, we may be less apt to turn to her for fashion tips. Bob may be a good accountant/tax man, but you wouldn't ask him where to go on vacation. Sally may be a good source for what's "in" in the fashion world, but she couldn't help you decide how to bet on this weekend's football game.

TRY THIS: Assemble Your Board of Directors

Make a list of the people you'd like to have on your board. Unlike the exercise in Chapter 5 about modeling, these advisors should be real people to whom you have access. The topics below will help you begin thinking about the different opinion leaders who affect your life.

Who would you go to for advice about:

1. Politics (local or national)
2. Investments
3. Real estate or homebuilding ideas
4. Clothing styles
5. Movies
6. Sports
7. Home repairs (divide this into different types)
8. Computers
9. Career planning
10. Restaurants

(Add at least three more categories)

Building "Win-Win" Relationships

"You can have everything you want in life if you'll just help others get what they want," believes Zig Ziglar.

Networking with the sincere intent of seeking out what is mutually helpful to you and others is critical to bouncing back. For many people, slumps and setbacks are rooted in selfishness or, at least, self-centeredness.

When we feel depressed, it is not unusual to focus inward, to feel sorry for ourselves, and to shut out others.

When we are low in spirit, we want to be alone or to commiserate with others who are also depressed. But doing so is counterproductive. As the proverb says, "If you always live with those who are lame, you will yourself learn to limp."

Now is the time to build or strengthen your support network. Now is the time to seek "win-win" opportunities and go after them. Now is the time to help someone else. When we help another we help ourselves.

Helen, for example, was experiencing a severe slump. Her family included three teenagers, one of whom had made a series of poor choices and was now paying the consequences for his actions. A once happy family was now rocked by problems with drugs, dishonesty, and constant disagreements. Helen felt that her world was coming apart. The model family she thought she had been rearing was becoming a problem family. All family relationships were strained. Helen felt that she was somehow responsible for the whole mess.

After months of feeling discouraged and frustrated, Helen made a good decision. She vowed that she would no longer allow the actions of one family member to disrupt the rest of the family and consume all her time and emotional energy. She began paying more attention to her other children and even got back into her habit of visiting an elderly friend in a nursing home. She decided to look beyond herself and create a "win-win" situation by serving others.

It worked. Family problems did not suddenly disappear, but Helen became more content when she saw that she was still a person of great worth—someone needed and loved. Visiting her bed-ridden friend made her count her own blessing of good health. Spending time with her friends, instead of tuning them out as she had for many months, quickly revealed that many families faced problems with wayward teenagers and that support systems were available to them through classes and group therapy. By communicating openly and authentically, she found the support she needed.

Each of us can build a support network through communicating authentically with ourselves and others.

Specific Behaviors for "Win-Win" Strategy
(☑ Check off when you've tried them)

☐ 1. Listen with a new level of awareness to the ways you communicate with yourself. Look for flaws of reasoning and language. Analyze how you use language and make it a goal to reduce or eliminate those words and expressions that are counterproductive.

☐ 2. Read at least one good book or listen to at least one good tape on interpersonal communication. Resolve to apply those techniques that will help strengthen relationships with others.

☐ 3. Review the activities in this chapter. Give special thought to assembling your board of directors. Talk to each member of the board and tell each why you respect and value their advice. Inquire if they feel comfortable about serving you in this way. Carry their names and phone numbers with you in your planner. Then do all you can to strengthen your relationships with them.

BEST IDEA 5

Stick With It

CHAPTER 8

APPLYING THE RITUALS OF WINNERS _____

If all we needed were ideas and positive thinking, then we all would have had our ponies when we were kids and we would all be living our "dream life" now. Action is what unites every great success.
—Anthony Robbins in *Unlimited Power*

Persistence is the greatest of all the power sources. By determinedly applying what we know to be useful, we can and will achieve our realistic goals.
—Author

This book is based on the premise that by applying basic and established success habits, we can and will bounce back from any slump or setback. You have undoubtedly already tried some of the ideas presented in this book. Perhaps you experienced positive results, perhaps not. People have come up to me in seminars and said, "I tried that imaging idea, and it didn't do a thing for me," or, "I used to keep a goal planner but didn't see any big difference in my life."

Perhaps so. But before I discount the wisdom of the many sources who have studied successful people, I ask one more question: "For how long did you try it?"

"Oh, I tried imaging two or three times and nothing happened." "I used a planner for a week and it didn't work." These responses overlook a fundamental fact: Changing human behavior takes time. You became the way you are today as a result of the sum of your experiences through your entire life up until now. If you are frustrated because you are overweight, consider how long it took you to reach this size. If you are irritated at yourself because of your procrastination, think about how long it took you to master the art of procrastination!

Anthony Robbins writes, "There are no failures, only *outcomes*. If you shot at a target and missed, you didn't fail, you just hit something else. If you tried to start a business but did not make any money at it, you didn't fail, you just created a different outcome: poverty. If you tried to run five miles but walked the last two, you didn't fail, you just produced a result different from what you had intended."

It does no good to flog yourself for failures, because there *are* no failures. If you reframe negative experiences as outcomes different from what you had planned, you can look back objectively and consider what you did to create that particular outcome. If you want a different outcome, do things differently next time.

In order to bounce back, you need to create some different habits of thought and action. In this final chapter, I will focus on four habits that will help you to do so:

1. The habit of feeling good,
2. The habit of staying balanced,
3. The habit of being patient, and
4. The habit of being appreciative.

The Habit of Feeling Good

Is feeling good really a habit? It can be, when you learn to control and discipline your mind and body. When you feel good, you work well. When you work well, you accomplish the things that are important to you.

Two aspects of feeling good can make an enormous difference in your ability to bounce back. First, I will discuss negative stress—that ever-present, aggravating disease of modern times. Then, I'll address the connection between our physical well-being and mental outlook.

Stress and Distress: Considering the Primal Scream

While stress is inevitable, it is certainly controllable. To the degree that we learn how to respond to stress positively, we greatly enhance our chances for success. As Thomas Jefferson said, "Nothing gives one person so much advantage over another as to remain always cool and unruffled under all circumstances."

Every human being experiences some stress in daily life. Potential stressors are everywhere: barking dogs, grouchy bosses, demanding children, frustrating work situations, and an inability to control aspects of our personal life are some of them. Let's take a look at an example.

It's a bright, sunny morning as Erika leaves her home and starts her three-month-old car to drive to work. She always wanted a sports car and she loves this little, red Thunderfire roadster. As she backs down the driveway, she both feels and hears a disconcerting "thump, thump." She stops the car and discovers an eight-penny nail sticking out of one of the rear tires. She mutters, "Why me? These are brand new radial tires. That stupid carpenter working next door must have dropped that nail. Why does this have to happen to me; I'm going to end up being late for work!" Diligently, she jacks up the car and changes the tire, getting grease on her new slacks in the process.

Finally, on the road to work, Erika stops at an intersection and waits for the light to turn green. Suddenly her head snaps back as someone crunches into her rear bumper. The damage is minor. While Erika and the offending motorist exchange names and addresses, the other driver remarks: "Boy, I'm sure glad I ran into you. Would you like to go to Disco 53 with me tonight?" After an icy, "No thank you," Erika begins to wonder if she will ever get to work. Finally, she makes it, 20 minutes late. Her boss says, "Nice of you to join us today, Ms. Wilson." He looks at his watch and turns away.

With stomach churning, Erika goes to her office, where she notes a stack of papers and books that need to be reviewed immediately.

She's relieved to be at work and happy that her appointment schedule is light. She says to herself, "Well, at least I'll be able to dig in and get this work finished." No sooner has that thought crossed her mind when her boss sticks his head through the door and says, "Sorry to interrupt you, Erika. I know you planned on catching up on some paperwork today, but a problem has come up at the plant." Erika rushes to the plant where she has several unpleasant encounters with an obstinate union leader, and a disenchanted employee who claims that management isn't concerned about factory safety, fair wages, truth, justice, or the American way.

Following lunch, Erika returns to her office, ready to dive into the stack of paperwork, when the phone rings. It's her mother. "Hi dear," she begins. "You're not going to believe this, but I fell down and hurt my leg. Could you come quickly and take me to the doctor's? I do hate to bother you, but I'm sitting outside a pay phone on 54th and Biscayne Drive."

After getting Mom to the hospital, Erika rushes back to her office. She realizes that she doesn't have time to complete her work. Everyone is heading for home, and the janitor wants to wax the floor tonight. She gives up, tosses her work in a briefcase, and goes to her car. When she arrives home, her sister Vera greets her with more news—their mother's leg was broken, the insurance policy covers only half of the medical costs, and the doctor bills and cast will total $570. Without comment, Erika sighs to herself, walks into the family room, and turns on the TV in hopes of forgetting what is happening to her.

Although few of us have days that feature this many distressing experiences, many of us have unpleasant experiences all too frequently. Our stomachs churn, we worry, we wonder what we can do to get our work done, and we question why everything seems to happen to us. Such reactions are normal.

The Difference between Distress and Stress

We need to distinguish between "distress" and "stress." Erika experiences some *severe* distress. And, although this is related to stress, distress is a primarily negative form of stress—acute mental or physical suffering that causes anxiety, strain, sorrow, or discomfort.

Stress is a more neutral condition. It can be damaging *or* useful, depending upon one's attitude toward it. A five o'clock deadline for a report may inflame one worker's ulcer but provide a helpful motivator for a colleague. We alone determine whether an experience is distressful (painful, anxiety-producing, etc.) or *merely* stressful.

Another example: A confrontation with another person can be emotionally hurtful or rewarding. The statement, "I'm glad we got our differences out in the open" may express a positive outcome to stress.

The point here is that all forms of stress—physical, mental, or emotional tension—need not be distressful. Indeed, just as muscles are strengthened by exposing them to the stress of exertion, so do we temper and toughen our mental and emotional selves by experiencing stress. It helps to take the mental outlook that not all stress is bad. Indeed, a stress-free world would be extremely dull—and the dullness would quickly become distressing!

Mastering the Art of the Mellow

When you set high standards for yourself and are working hard to align your goals, values, and daily activities, stress can seem as much a part of your life as eating or breathing—so much so that you don't even realize that you're feeling it. We live in a society addicted to efficiency and speed—we're constantly on the phone, in meetings, flying off to various parts of the world to meet clients, and so forth. Even leisure time is often spent networking in the gym, taking courses to learn new skills, or working to reinforce your self-concept. It's hardly surprising that you feel you have no free time.

It doesn't have to be this way, however. Learning to relax will not only help you to create a more serene and enjoyable life, it's also the key to being more productive with the time that you do have. A recent article in *Working Woman* magazine strongly recommends that we understand what stress does to our body and meet it head on with "active" relaxation. What that entails is making a concentrated effort to take time out *every* day to do something that calms you.

Your company may have health and fitness programs. But whether or not you have access to such a program, the major promise you have to make is to yourself. Active relaxation gives you ways to make your life your own. Learning to relax through active relaxation can make your bad days easier to survive and your good days better than ever.

Exercising Stress Away

Have you experienced a relaxed, mellow feeling after working out? It's not all in your head. Recent research proves that specific physiological changes occur in your body when you exercise and that they may temper or even override the ravages of stress. What's more, there's evidence that being aerobically fit can make stress easier to handle.

Kenneth Cooper, M.D., founder of the Institute for Aerobic Research in Dallas, has pointed out that people who are aerobically fit have lower heart rates during stress periods than people who aren't fit. A fit body doesn't release as many hormones in response to stress, so there aren't as many chemicals floating around in the system and your body can more quickly return to normal. A good workout also causes you to release betaendorphins—the powerful, morphine-like substances that have been linked to that feeling of well-being known as "runner's high."

These endorphins make you feel good. In fact, our body enjoys the endorphins so much that well-conditioned people who stop exercising experience withdrawal symptoms—they get crabby and uncomfortable if they miss working out for a few days. Being addicted to endorphins is a healthy, natural "addiction."

Dr. Cooper says that when you work out on a regular basis, more endorphins get into your system in a shorter amount of time and stay there longer.

Interestingly, if you don't regularly exercise, your body responds by increasing endorphin levels *after* a workout—too late to derive maximum benefit. In other words, if you are out of shape and you work out too hard, the endorphins come out after the workout and serve merely as an anesthetic to dull the pain that untoned muscles and ligaments experience.

The object of a physical workout is to get your heart rate into its training zone, (that is, between 60 and 80 percent of 220 beats per minute minus your age) for 30-40 minutes at least three times a week.

TRY THIS: Calculate Your Training Zone

The best aerobic effect is achieved from exercise that raises your heartbeat up to the level optimum for you. To calculate your training zone:

    (a) Subtract your age from 220   = _____
    (b) Multiply (a) by .60   = _____
    (c) Now multiply (a) by .80   = _____

Your ideal training zone is found between these two numbers. If you are just starting out, raise your heart rate to the (b) level and keep it there for 15-20 minutes. As you progress, you may increase within your training zone.

Aerobic fitness can be achieved by several activities. Jogging is popular with many people, although some who fear damage to joints have switched to brisk walking. Swimming and cycling are also recommended. You don't have to go fast. Doctors agree that the more you work out aerobically, the more fit you become, and the more fit you are, the better you can handle stress.

> **TRY THIS:**   **Using Endorphins**
>
> Be sure to check with your doctor before starting a strenuous exercise program. When you have worked up a good sweat in an aerobic exercise, cool down with imaging. I often do my positive imaging after a vigorous physical workout. The endorphins have already helped me relax, allowing me to enter a hypnotic state very quickly. Then, I can use my affirmations and other techniques discussed in Chapter 5 to reap maximum benefit from imaging.

Another Way to Handle Stress: Releasing the Pressure

While exercise is an excellent way to cope with some kinds of stress, other techniques can be used effectively, too. Since life is made up of an accumulation of distressors—some large, some small—that can undermine your health and well-being, we need specific techniques for releasing them. What can you do to relieve the pressure these stresses place upon your mind and body? Try using a technique called "releasing the pressure." Releasing is like letting air out of a balloon before it pops.

When we learn to release, we gain control of a process that may have happened to you inadvertently. For example, perhaps you were in the middle of an argument when you suddenly stopped and thought, "Wait a minute. What am I doing? This isn't that important!" At the time, your perspective took a 180 degree turn, and you were then better able to cope with the other person. You let the air out of the balloon before it popped. Remember, you choose to allow the pressures mount and you can also choose to let go of the distress. You release the pressure.

Or perhaps you were trying to meet a tough deadline and the nearer it came, the more inefficient you grew. As your tension mounted, maybe you said to yourself, "Why am I getting so worked up?" At that point, your sense of urgency melted away, and you were able to regroup and mobilize your energies effectively. As in the example of the person who could not sleep the night before an important meeting, trying too hard just makes things worse. You cannot will yourself to sleep until you have released your anxiety about sleeping.

In each of these instances, letting go of feelings that are preoccupying and consuming you changes your perception of the event and thereby reduces your stress.

When used deliberately, releasing can make for rapid, on-the-spot change. It is simple, takes seconds to accomplish, and can diffuse problems and stress moment by moment in your life.

Key to releasing pressure is to stop *pushing*. When frustrated, we often feel driven to do better, to succeed at all cost. If the problem fails to yield to our pushing, we often assume that the solution is to push harder—much harder.

But this can be self-defeating. In fact, it almost invariably makes matters worse. Surprisingly enough, when we *stop* our pushing, new options present themselves and the situation becomes manageable. Releasing the need for a solution allows one to emerge naturally.

The problem with pushing stems from the difference between physical and mental work. Remember, psychologists have found that when working with intellectual problems or concerns (planning, problem solving, etc.) we are almost inevitably more effective when we relax than when we exert ourselves. Of course, this contrasts with physical work. In addressing a physical task, the more force we apply, the more effective we are.

Releasing is a particularly useful stress reduction technique. Sometimes, we simply need to back off and say, "So what? Is is it really going to be the end of the world if I miss this deadline by a few minutes or a few hours?" "Why have I set this specific target for myself? Is it *that* important?" Stop and take an objective look at what you're doing and determine whether or not it really *is* that important.

Sometimes, we also need to use the release technique to cope with events that have already happened. We can imagine the event in the present and release it. Think back on a situation where you were insulted or upset. Think it through again, as though it's happening now, and determine how to release it from your mind.

TRY THIS: **A Releasing Review**

To use releasing for maximum effectiveness, conduct a releasing review at the end of each day to neutralize stressors that have slipped by unnoticed. Find a quiet place and let your mind roam over the day's events, catching those still unsolved and releasing them as they surface.

The Habit of Staying Balanced

A second way to court success is by creating balance in our lives.

Earlier, I presented six categories that define success for most people. We succeed to the degree that we have achieved satisfactory levels of each of these categories:

1. *Peace of mind.* We feel confident that our basic needs will be met. We're going to have enough food to eat and air to breathe and opportunities available to make our lives worth living.

2. *Health and vigor.* No one is *always* healthy, and some of us are physically challenged or have problematic physical conditions. The degree to which we achieve a sense of satisfaction about our health and our degree of vigor is a measure of our success. If we are constantly worried or preoccupied about our health, it is very difficult to achieve our goals.

3. *Loving relationships.* Relationships are critical to our success. No man is an island, and no one can truly be successful without building and nurturing relationships with others. Human beings are social animals. Some of us may prefer on occasion to work alone, but all of us have an innate need for loving relationships. Without those relationships, we cannot be successful.

4. *Financial freedom.* This does not necessarily mean that we are rich and can buy anything we want. Rather, it means we have achieved sufficient economic resources that we are not consumed with worry or anxiety about from where our next dollar is coming. We have enough money to meet our basic needs and are not excessively anxious about where our funding will come from in the future.

5. *Worthy goals and ideals.* Human beings seek goals, striving constantly to improve, grow, and learn. To the extent that we do so and project ourselves toward worthwhile goals and ideals, we are successful.

6. *Feelings of personal fulfillment.* It is important to create situations in which we can experience success. For truly, success breeds success. To the degree that we experience personal fulfillment and feel ourselves growing, we are indeed successful.

We measure success in terms of how we're doing with respect to each of these six characteristics. It is important to note that we are our sole judge in these matters. The outside world cannot really know how successful we are, for our success can be measured by us alone.

In the early 1980's, Jessica Savitch was one of television's most prominent newscasters. In 1982, a *TV Guide* poll named her the fourth most trusted anchor on television news.

Her history in the industry was impressive. In the early 1960's, she got her first job at the age of fourteen working at a New Jersey radio station. She moved up in the broadcasting industry and became "a major success story."

Several years after her tragic death in an automobile accident in 1983, more information about Jessica Savitch has come to light. And the picture is now very different. While Jessica had made impressive professional achievements—coming close to the top of her profession with a fabulous network news job and a staggering salary, her personal life was apparently in considerable disarray. She was very unhappy before her tragic death at the age of 36.

It is not my intent to pass judgment on Jessica Savitch, but to make the point that someone who appears to be very successful to those of us on the outside looking in, may, in fact, have huge problems.

TRY THIS: **How Are You Doing?**

Rate your current level of success in each of the six categories. Remember, success is the degree to which *you are satisfied with your progress*, not some absolute level of achievement. Use a scale of one to 10, with one at the bottom and 10 at the top.

1. *Peace of Mind:*   1 —————— 5 —————— 10

2. *Health and Vigor*   1 —————— 5 —————— 10

3. *Loving Relationships*   1 —————— 5 —————— 10

4. *Financial Freedom*   1 —————— 5 —————— 10

5. *Worthy Goals*   1 —————— 5 —————— 10

6. *Personal Fulfillment*   1 —————— 5 —————— 10

The Habit of Patient Self-Discipline

Self-control takes self-discipline. And self-discipline demands *patience* as we diligently pursue our goals.

To some people, self-discipline connotes punishment, but it is just the opposite. It is the very quality that sets us free and permits us joy in our accomplishments.

In a tape program called *The Neuropschology of Self-Discipline* by SyberVision Corporation, Steven DeVore points out 10 characteristics of self-disciplined achievers. Paraphrasing DeVore's descriptions, self-disciplined achievers possess the following characteristics:

1. *A strong, well-defined sense of purpose; they know what they want.* It is critical to identify core values and determine exactly what we really want from life. Once we have identified our values and suitable value-aligning activities, we should pursue them single-mindedly.

Ironically, people who lack a sense of direction, perhaps preferring to "leave their options open," are really only leaving open the option of failure. It is impossible to be successful without having a strong sense of purpose.

2. *Positive role models or mentors.* General George Patton is a hero in motivational literature as he was on the battlefield. Undoubtedly, many cadets at the U.S. Military Academy would love to become just like Patton. But Patton, too, had a mentor; he had studied in depth the works and writings of Alexander the Great. This ruler became a mentor for Patton. Patton got to the point where he could think like Alexander the Great and achieved some of the kinds of battle victories that Alexander the Great had achieved.

Each of us needs to look around to see what mentors or role models we can identify with and model ourselves after. Discipline yourself to identify people, whether real or imaginary, living or dead, who can provide role models for you. They can become your mentors. Look at them and say, "If they can do it, I can do it." Then find out how they did it, and do it yourself!

3. *A powerful imagination.* We've learned that producing clear, constructive images in our minds can help us achieve great things. For many people, reaching a particular goal seems almost *deja vu.* Upon realizing their goal, they have the strange sensation that they've been there before. In a sense, they have, for they've already lived that success mentally.

4. *A positive sensory orientation.* Such people have an optimistic view of the world. This positive mental attitude and belief in oneself helps us achieve the things we want to do.

Other psychologists speak of the "locus of control" where some people feel that their life can be controlled from within while others feel that their life is controlled largely by forces outside of themselves. Highly disciplined achievers know that much of what happens in life is within their control and they possess a positive sensory orientation.

On the other hand, people with a negative sensory orientation, view the world through pessimistic eyes. They focus on limitations, drawbacks, and impossibilities instead of possibilities. Such people cannot succeed because they have fixated on the negative, blocking out the positive. The mind cannot dwell on negatives and achieve positives.

5. *Self-confidence and a belief in their ability to achieve.* The notion that we must develop a sense of self-confidence, high self-esteem, a general feeling that we like and trust ourselves, feel good about our capabilities, and are making progress toward our goals and objectives is critical to being successful. Disciplined achievers possess these beliefs in abundance, *and they take specific steps to foster and nurture these beliefs.*

6. *Planning and organizing skills.* Disciplined achievers can set a large goal and then very carefully plan how to achieve it by accomplishing specific tasks. They know the priorities of these tasks and move ahead in a systematic way to achieve them.

7. *Acquire essential knowledge and skills and put them to work.* An important difference between one who simply dreams about success and one who achieves it is that the achiever will work to acquire the tools needed, the essential knowledge and skills required to make achievement a reality. For some people, this means going back to school, taking seminars, listening to tape programs, reading books. For others, it means taking short-term job opportunities to learn some of the needed skills. Many large corporations will have their most promising executives work in various areas throughout the company. Even the top executives at McDonald's Corporation, for example, know how to cook a Big Mac and clean a kitchen in a McDonald's restaurant. They've learned all the skills necessary to be successful in their business by rotating from position to position throughout the organization.

8. *Patience.* Things take time. One of the problems for those who lack discipline is that they want everything *now* and demand immediate gratification. This is rarely the way things work in life. To those who are dedicated to pursuing a goal, time is virtually immaterial because getting there is half the fun. If our objective is truly worthwhile, we will enjoy spending the time necessary to achieve it.

9. *Persistence.* Good habits, those rituals performed day after day, are the most critical tools to reaching our goals and objectives. Persistence always pays when used in pursuit of a worthwhile goal.

10. *Pleasure while working to achieve their vision.* All gratification need not be deferred until the goal is reached. If a goal is truly worthwhile and something that really interests us, getting there will be fun. The disciplined achiever knows that making progress—even minor improvements in the desired direction—is both rewarding and enjoyable.

TRY THIS: Inventory for the Self-Disciplined Achiever

This might be a good time to take an inventory to determine to what extent you share these 10 characteristics with the high achiever. Following is a quiz where you can rate yourself to see just how you're doing. Use a 1-10 scale, with 10 the highest rating. Areas in which you score lowest are potentially the most fruitful ones in which to concentrate your efforts.

1. Define a strong sense of purpose.   1 — 5 — 10

2. Seek out positive role models/mentors.   1 — 5 — 10

3. Possess a vivid imagination.   1 — 5 — 10

4. Possess a positive sensory orientation.   1 — 5 — 10

5. Believe in your ability to achieve.   1 — 5 — 10

6. Plan and organize.   1 — 5 — 10

---

7. Acquire needed knowledge and skills.	1 — 5 — 10
8. Be patient.	1 — 5 — 10
9. Be persistent.	1 — 5 — 10
10. Experience pleasure while working.	1 — 5 — 10

Based on this self-evaluation, which areas require the most work now?

The realm of physical fitness provides good examples of self-discipline. In fact, it is in this area that we probably have the most control over what happens to us.

Let's Get Physical

For many people, building the habit of patient self-discipline starts with the physical aspects of their lives. They lack the health, vigor, stamina, or personal appearance that they would like, and yet they find it very difficult to do what's necessary for improvement.

Being overweight is a problem of epidemic proportions among Americans. Some 59 million Americans (about one in four) are on a weight loss diet right now. At no time in history have people had so much food available to them and so many conveniences that reduce the need for physical exercise. One result has been that many men and women are overweight. Let's take the example of Tamera.

Tamera is about 35 pounds overweight and uncomfortable associating with others because she knows she does not look as good as she could. Tamera gained much of her excess weight in the last few years. When she occasionally encounters people who knew her when she was slender, they often express surprise to see how large she's become. What could Tamera do about being fat?

First, she needs to decide if she *truly* has a sense of purpose, if she cares enough to become trim. Secondly, she needs to seek out some positive role models and see how they eat and exercise.

Tamera could certainly use imaging to create a sensory vision of what it would be like to be slender again. To have the lean body that she used to have she might do things as simple as look at old photographs of herself when she was in better shape and display them to remind herself of what she could once again look like. Tamera also needs to keep a positive sensory orientation, to believe in herself and have confidence that since she was slender at one time, there's no reason why she cannot be slender again.

As Tamera begins to lose weight and engage in more vigorous physical activity, she will bolster her belief in herself. Her self-esteem about her physical characteristics will rise.

Tamera could benefit from planning and organizing, setting goals in her weight-control program. She might set a target, establish some short-term goals about how she will eat, and write in her planner specific activities to engage in each day as she strives to reduce her weight and attain a better physical condition.

Certainly, Tamera can acquire knowledge and skill to help her lose weight and get back into shape. Many diet and exercise programs are effective when patiently and persistently followed. Typical fad diets and quick fix programs that promise rapid weight loss are ineffective and actually result in weight gain, making things worse than they were before.

If we were to watch Tamara get her weight under control and build a lean, healthy body, we could see that being a disciplined achiever can bring about beautiful results!

Patience, Self-discipline, and the Uncontrollable

Career slumps or setbacks can be the result of many factors beyond our control. If our company is bought out or technological change makes our job obsolete, what then?

We can use the same approaches discussed throughout this book. We go back to basics and *persistently* apply success principles day after day until we've solved our problem. Because we have less direct control, we need additional faith. We have faith that the chair we are sitting on will hold us, that the sky will not fall, and that the laws of physics and chemistry will prevail.

Similarly, we need to exercise faith that what actions we use to bounce back will work. And they will. Especially when we bring to them one final habit:

The Habit of Being Patiently Appreciative

As the Bible says, we should "run the race with patience," having faith that we will be justly rewarded for our efforts. Young people have an especially difficult time doing this. But for those of us who have been riding life's roller coaster for a few years, the concept becomes more valid.

If a child plants seeds in his garden but digs them up every few days to see how they're coming along, the likelihood of producing mature plants is slim. But often, we don't give things enough time to germinate. We want results and we want them *now*!

It's not surprising that so many people lack patience. We live in a world where problems are solved in 30 seconds on TV commercials and a few hours in a movie. Seldom does anyone remind us that real life runs slower. Some problems take years to solve. But solved they will be, *if* we have the patience to pursue their solutions.

People who play the stock market looking for the quick hit almost always lose in the long run, while conservative investors seeking slow but steady appreciation almost always come out ahead.

A mighty canyon is carved out by the relentless trickle of tiny droplets of water.

We are all richly blessed by providence. Regardless of your religious convictions, it makes sense to be thankful for all that you already have. Striving for different and better circumstances is a normal human endeavor. But being thankful for what we already have is the mark of the fulfilled person.

Here is one more brief exercise worthy of regular repetition:

> **TRY THIS:**   **Count Your Blessings**
>
> Take a few moments and list as many blessings as you can. Your health, family, relationships, career, opportunities, and freedoms are matters to consider; make as long a list as possible. The next time you feel really down and out, reread the list or, better yet, write a new one.

I believe that those who appreciate what they have, receive more. Those who fail to appreciate what they have, get less.

The Four "R's" of Any Success System

There are four major components to any success system, including this one, to help you bounce back. They are also found in all major religions. Think for a moment about your involvement with the four "R's":

1. *Rituals.* In religions, these are the ceremonies that are observed regularly to remind us of significant religious truths. In our success system, they are our routine activities to advance us toward desired goals and values. Daily planning, regular imaging, use of affirmations, and value shaping are examples of such rituals.

2. *Restrictions.* In religions, these are the prohibitions that instruct us in what to avoid. In our success system, they are also the limits beyond which you decide you will not trespass. For example, you may make a commitment that "I will not be away from family more than a few days a month," or "I will never associate with an organization that employs unethical or shady practices," or "I will not work for a producer of a product that is harmful to people or the environment," etc.

3. *Regulations.* In religions, these are the commandments that encourage us to do positive acts, such as honoring our parents, contributing to the needy, attending services, loving our neighbors, etc. In our success system, they are the value-aligning activities that move us toward value congruence.

4. *Relationships.* The outcome of the first three "R's" affects the fourth. We become more caring for others as we grow and succeed. We recognize that little can be accomplished without others' cooperation and help. And in the long run, no accomplishment can compensate for destroyed relationships. Relationships are the ultimate end of our existence, for we are commanded above all to love one another.

Now, it's time for you to bounce back.

Specific Behaviors You Can Use to Apply the Rituals of Winners
(☑ Check them off as you complete them)

☐ 1. Make a commitment to learn more about stress management. Keep in mind that stress is not all bad and, in fact, can be useful.

☐ 2. If you are not already doing so, begin an aerobic exercise program appropriate for you. Don't overdo it, and do get medical advice, but start today to become more physically fit.

☐ 3. Review the section on life balance. Now draw a hub with six equal spokes. Assume that each spoke represents a 1-to-10 evaluation of how well you are doing in this dimension of success. Place a mark on each spoke to reflect your level of accomplishment. Now draw a circular line to connect the points you've marked. Is your wheel round or lopsided? If it's lopsided (and most are), how can you bring it back into balance?

☐ 4. Read the Epilogue to see what happened to our fictional characters from the opening stories.

EPILOGUE

EPILOGUE

CLASSIC CAREER SLUMPERS REVISITED

Bill and **Linda Chandler**—remember them?—both stared silently at the TV. That's about as close to communicating as they got these days. Bill's eyes shifted momentarily to the stack of today's mail as he snapped his beer can open, a nonverbal sign to let the kids know that they had better keep away from him tonight. Among the stack of bills, a brightly colored catalog caught his eye and, for a moment, his interest.

"What's that?" Linda asked.

"Some ad for motivational tapes or something, I guess. Of course, I don't need anything like that. I'm about as motivated as that lamp over there," Bill replied sarcastically.

The catalog promised "unlimited possibilities," "success breakthroughs," and more. Its illustrations showed people who seemed to be living the kind of life Bill and Linda had always assumed they'd live. Bill laughed bitterly at the thought of driving a luxury car or living in a nice, big house or owning his own business. Then he picked up the catalog and looked a little closer. He felt his heart jump just a bit. THE SLUMP had forcefully taught him never to chase pipe dreams, yet every once in a while he could still vaguely see himself running his own architectural firm.

"How much are these tapes, anyhow? Gee, they don't seem too expensive. What have I got to lose. Maybe I'll try a set, just this once."

That was a little over three years ago. They've been challenging years—in a good sense. Once Bill decided it was time to bounce back, he spent some time clarifying his life values. Then he got serious about controlling his time and efforts, and things started to fall into place. Bill put in long hours of hard work. And he had made major progress toward his life-long goals. He completed his schooling and was invited by his uncle in Chicago to join the firm as a partner.

Linda began reading and listening to motivational programs, too. In fact, they both became self-improvement "junkies" and regularly attend success seminars. For the past year, Linda has been managing a retail sales network selling a quality line of jewelry and sweaters. In fact, she wrote a computer program that lets her keep track of the sales, commissions, inventory, and billings for the 12 distributors who report to her and for more than 50 others reporting to her distributors.

Bill and Linda changed their lives by changing their habits. The motivational tapes didn't do it; they did it. The tapes just showed the way, provided a blueprint etched by those who've gone before. Bill and Linda's dream wasn't really dead. It was just in a coma.

Frank Baker's story also took a promising turn. His wife, Donna, became increasingly concerned about Frank's behavior. She suggested that he see a doctor, which he grudgingly did. The doctor immediately suggested that Frank try an antidepressant medication. Frank tried to explain that he "doesn't do drugs," but the doctor and Donna talked him into using the medication for a while "to see if it helps."

Frank had displayed classic symptoms of depression: apathy, frustration, compulsive behaviors (his constant running), and even thoughts of suicide. The doctor explained that depression can often be brought on by emotional stress. Pushing oneself too hard to achieve professional goals—especially those dictated by other people—is terribly stressful, for example. And after months or years of such pressure, a chemical imbalance in the brain can result. If this occurs, a combination of counseling and medication seems to be most helpful.

Frank's doctor gave him a five-page brochure about depression, and Frank began to realize that he was not crazy, but ill. The medication took about a week to make any difference, but when it kicked in, the results were dramatic. One morning, Frank woke up and felt almost like his old self again. He was cheerful, easy to get along with, and optimistic.

There continued to be good and bad days, but the good ones began to outnumber the bad. Frank found his moods much more even. He started using imaging regularly and received solid insight about what he should be doing and where he should go.

His career changed somewhat, too. He decided to pursue a different teaching emphasis in his work at the university. He became genuinely excited about entrepreneurship and wrote a book on the subject. He also explained his newly clarified values and goals to his boss, the dean of the college, and found a supportive, caring ally. The dean soon suggested that Frank develop the school's first course in entrepreneurship, a project Frank attacked with enthusiasm.

Frank's relationship with his wife, family, and friends bounced back, too. He shed his image as a grouch and returned to being the genuinely likeable guy he had been in the past. This occurred as he found renewed direction in his life and his self-esteem rose.

Slowly, life took on new meaning again. It was even fun! Frank realized that what he had gone through was not unusual. A number of his close friends confided to him that they, too, had had a similar slump. The mid-life muddle is no more unusual for middle-agers than the symptoms of adolescence are for teenagers. For some in both categories, it reaches crisis proportions with serious mistakes made. For many, it is simply a passage through another phase of life, one to be learned from, not cursed.

Frank Baker is now a fully functioning, active professional, who senses a heightened awareness of what life is really about and what is truly important to him. He has prevailed and triumphed—and is the richer for his wealth of experience, however painfully acquired.

Anita Cushman bounced back, too. After months of regret and resentment, she decided that that wasn't how she wanted to spend the rest of her life. Resentment does nothing but fester. Instead, she began working to release her animosity and select a new opportunity.

Anita decided to tap the network of associations she had developed over the years. She contacted past employees whom she had helped. She created a "board of directors" with a publisher friend as chairman.

As she worked on value clarification and imaging, it became increasingly clear to her that she gained tremendous satisfaction from teaching people but that seminars and individual coaching were not the only ways to teach. She focused her attention on writing several workbooks that were adopted by a training department at a local bank.

Then, one day, seemingly by coincidence, she received a call from a videotape producer who had come across her workbook and wondered is she'd like to make it into a video. Her power to reach others had just taken a quantum leap!

Over a period of three years, Anita has created and appeared in six video training programs, each paying her a handsome royalty. She now devotes all her work time to writing and research, and she works at home. She loves it. The headaches of the training business, with all its logistical problems, are almost forgotten. So, too, is the resentment she felt toward the people who acquired her company.

Besides, now that she works at home, she sets her own hours without feeling pressured by others. She finds that she now has time to work as a volunteer, teaching adult reading skills, which gives her enormous satisfaction.

Financially, professionally, and personally, Anita has not just bounced back. She has far exceeded her previous level of life satisfaction.

How will your story unfold?

Only you can write those chapters. I would like to think that the ideas in this book will help make the challenge enticing and the outcome satisfying.

The techniques of success are neither mysterious nor obscure. Indeed, never before has a formula for bouncing back been more readily available. The principles worked for the Chandlers, the Bakers, Anita Cushman, and thousands of people like you and me.

Apply the FIVE BEST IDEAS over a reasonable period of time and you'll bounce back, too.

THE FIVE BEST IDEAS (One More Time)

1. LIKE YOURSELF

2. DO THE RIGHT THINGS

3. DO THINGS RIGHT

4. TREAT PEOPLE WELL

5. STICK WITH IT

Order Form for The *Plan-It Life Organizer*©

To order your *Plan-It Life Organizer*©, send your order to Crisp Publications, Inc., 95 First Street, Los Altos, CA 94022 or call (415) 949-4888.

The *Plan-It*© is 8½″ × 11″, standard 3-ring bind. It may be purchased with or without a binder. Retail costs are quoted below. Quantity discounts are available. Add $2.00 postage for each set ordered. California residents add appropriate tax.

One-year set of all pages	= $16.95
Index tabs	= $ 4.95
Binder (deluxe vinyl)	= $10.95

Quantity	*Description*	*Amount*
_____	_____	_____
_____	_____	_____
_____	_____	_____
	Postage and handling	_____
	California tax	_____
	TOTAL AMOUNT	_____

Ship To: _____

_____

_____

_____

Bill To: _____

_____

_____

_____

THE PAUL R. TIMM GROUP SELF-MANAGEMENT TRAINING

Self-management training seminars which expand on the materials in this book are available to organizations. For details contact the author, Dr. Paul R. Timm, at The Paul R. Timm Group, Inc., 81 E 2000 South, Orem, Utah 84058. Phone (801) 378-5682 or 226-0819.

©Paul R. Timm

Dear Reader—
Do any of these situations
sound familiar to you?

Item: "Downsizing" continues unabated...Fully 39 percent of 1,084 companies and nonprofit groups surveyed by the American Management Association cut work forces in the past year...
Item: More people than ever are taking the entrepreneurial route. Inherent with this is increased risk and the distinct possibility of setbacks...*Item:* The so-called "midlife crisis" is real. Just as surely as teenagers experience adolescence, men will experience a midlife slump that saps energy, creates depression, and causes them to conclude that they have failed—even when, in fact, they are very successful...
Item: Gone are the days when a student graduates, hires on with a big, secure company, and stays there through an orderly, satisfying career. Our world is one of constant changes...*Item:* Even in a period of economic recovery, job displacement is increasingly common. There is a one-in-10 chance that your job will disappear this year, according to the Bureau of Labor Statistics...*Item:* The causes of turbulence are many, but chief among them are such forces as new labor-saving technology, mergers, deregulation, foreign takeovers, restructurings, and a frenzy of cost cutting...*Item:* Major companies such as Ford and General Motors have announced their intentions to reduce white collar employment by 20 percent...*Item:* Displacement is likely to occur in giant corporations where job security was once taken for granted...*Item:* There is no longer any job security in the large companies...*Item:* Even when jobs seem secure, today's workers are increasingly restless, sensing that their work is far less fulfilling than it should be...There is a new ideal about work emerging: For the first time there is a widespread expectation that work should be fulfilling— that work should be fun. Thirty years ago, that would have been an outrageous notion. Nevertheless, people know intuitively that work ought to be fun and satisfying, even when it is not...

if so—
maybe it's time
for you to
RECHARGE YOUR CAREER
AND YOUR LIFE!

5510